Live Life Happy

One Day at a Time

Every day may not be good, but there is
something good every day.

Andrea Seydel

Copyright © 2021 by Andrea Seydel

All rights reserved.
Published and Distributed in Canada by LLH Publishing Inc.

www.andreaseydel.com[1]

Library of Congress Cataloging-in-Publication Data
Seydel, Andrea
Live Life Happy: One Day at a Time \ Andrea Seydel
1.Non Fiction Mental Health -2. Non-Fiction-Self-Help-Motivation & Inspiration
ISBN: 978-1-9991409-7-7

1st Printing: June 2021. Printed in Canada
Cover Photo Credit: Katie Burkhart
Proofreader: Lindy Bailey

Publisher's Note & Author DISCLAIMER
This publication is designed to provide accurate and authoritative information concerning the subject matter covered. It is sold to understand that the publisher and author are not engaging in or rendering any psychological, medical, or other professional services. If expert assistance or counselling is needed, seek the services of a competent medical professional. For immediate support, call your local crisis line.
BE WELL

Welcome:

Every day may not be good,
But there is something good in every day.

Rise and Shine. Each new day is a gift filled with possibilities. My mom woke me up every morning in my younger years, saying these phrases to me as we greeted the day. Still today, her loving voice and beautiful messages remain. Life is not always going to be sunshine and butterflies. It becomes essential to support your mental health and build resiliency.

What is exciting about life is that every morning offers a brand new day with unlimited possibilities. Yesterday's challenges and mistakes belong to yesterday while providing learning and growth. Today is a fresh, clean slate, a chance to start anew, to do or become anything you want. So jump into each day and Live Life Happy. This perpetual calendar brimming with engaging support is filled with daily encouragements and themes designed to enhance your well-being. This book combines the science of positive psychology and human resiliency with uplifting quotes and bite-size nuggets to help foster self-care, personal sustainability, and joy - because sometimes you might need reminders about how joyful and fun life can be!

Tap into your well-being and resilience -

One day at a time!

Hugs
Andrea

P.S. You can simply follow the dates in the book or flip through and randomly stop on a page for inspiration. The choice is yours!!

Andrea Seydel is a positive psychology practitioner, life coach, and educator who devotes her career to helping others Live Life Happy. She holds a degree in psychology with post-graduate studies in Positive Psychology, Non-Violent Communication, and Suicide Intervention. In addition, Andrea is a certified resilience and recovery coach and the host of The Live Life Happy Podcast. She can be reached at: www.andreaseydel.com

L

Live Life Happy

One Day at a Time

Every day may not be good, but there is
something good every day.

January 1

Hold comfort in your heart.

*"Whatever you're facing right now,
there's a way out."*
- Paul Jukes

Today's message
Take comfort knowing you are strong. Do what
brings comfort to your heart. Put your mind at ease
and trust that things will get better. If things seem
too challenging, think about a difficult time in the
past, and notice your strength in navigating the
struggle. There is evidence that tough times will
pass, and you will get through things. Take comfort
in knowing life isn't always going to be perfect.

Remember
Sometimes it is essential to remind yourself that
everything will be ok. Writing in a journal is a way of
talking to yourself without being interrupted. It is a
beautiful way to process emotions and understand
your thoughts. Think about what you need today.
Try to find things that bring you comfort and do
them during your times of struggle.

Ask yourself
What brings me peace? What gives me mental
clarity? What brings me comfort?

January 2

Take notice of friendship.

"The greatest healing therapy
is friendship and love."
- Hubert Humphrey

Today's message

Think about all the things that are going well for you right now and notice all the love surrounding you. It is up to you to believe and cherish those around you. Take the moments that you are in and make them meaningful. Reach out to others. Make time for the people in your life. Human connection and a sense of community are essential for your well-being. Talking with a friend or family member can offer an excellent source of strength. It is essential to be a friend to others as well. To have friends, you need to be a friend. Think about people you can call and connect with today. Choose to up the priority of friendships in your life. When you go through a struggle in life, which you inevitably will, your friends will offer you support and comfort through those trying times. It is also what they need when they are going through a struggle.

Ask yourself

Who are my good friends? Who can I reach out to and connect with today? Who helps and supports me along my path?

January 3

Enjoy gentle environments.

"There is nothing like staying at home for real comfort."
- Jane Austen

Today's message

Gentle people often treat others with kindness and a mild manner; you will need these people at certain times in your life. Be kind to yourself and learn to love who and what you are; forgive yourself. A peaceful environment starts with you. Retrain your mind to seek peace regularly. Surround yourself with warm and caring people that make you feel at ease. Choose to do things that are gentle and calming today. Calmness and gentleness soothe and calm your nervous system. Notice the people in your environment. Spend time in peaceful environments today. Look around and notice how you can make your environment more gentle and quieter. Notice your thoughts. How can you make your thoughts more soothing and gentler? You can influence your environment and choose where you want to be, what you want to focus on, and who you choose to be with. Choose gentleness today.

Affirm

I choose gentleness and peace in my life.
I listen to beautiful calming music.
I surround myself with beauty and calm.

January 4

Choose to find peace.

*"Forgive others, not because
they deserve forgiveness,
but because you deserve peace."*
- Jonathan Lockwood Huie

Today's message

Peace is the result of training and retraining your mind to interpret life as it is rather than how you think it should be. Don't let the bad behaviour of others destroy your sense of inner peace. Forgiveness is not for others but rather for you. It is about releasing any grievance story and retelling it with you as the hero instead of a victim. What grudge or grievance story have you been holding? As Fred Luskin, author of *Forgive for Good*, cleverly puts it: *forgiveness is the practice of extending your moments of peacefulness; forgiveness is the power that comes from knowing a past injustice does not have to hurt today*. Forgiveness is available anytime entirely under your control. It does not rely on the actions of others; it is a choice you alone can make.

Ask yourself

How can I stop fighting and taking things personally, and in doing so, find peace? Can I change the channel of my thinking to the joy, beauty, or love channel?

January 5

Be understanding with yourself.

"Don't just be good to others.
Be good to yourself too."
- Old Saying

Today's message

You deserve to have all the beautiful things in life. It's ok to focus on self-care and be selfish. Taking time to yourself will help you grow and learn. Being kind and understanding towards yourself is like being your own best friend. Nobody in life is perfect; it's essential not to be hard on yourself. Take time to listen to your needs, wants, and feelings today. Tap into things that you need, desire, and wish for today. Honour feelings that you might be having today. Offer yourself some compassion and grace. Without judgment, accept who you are and where you are today. Be grateful for the life you are living and the person you are today. Be good towards yourself. Just like you are kind to a best friend or loved one, be caring towards yourself today.

Ask yourself

How can I love myself unconditionally? What unrealistic standards am I holding? What am I needing, feeling, and wanting today? How can I offer myself support and kindness?

January 6

Trust that all is well.

"It's not the load that brings you down;
it's the way you carry it."
- Lou Holtz

Remember

Surrendering isn't about being passive. But it is about being open to possibilities beyond your control. When you surrender, you are letting go of the pressure and stress from trying to control situations that might be out of your control. Release the tension in your life by learning to let go of the things you cannot control or change. Your thoughts are powerful; be careful what thoughts you allow in your mind. When you shift the lens to a perspective of *all is well,* you will feel lighter and more peaceful. Sometimes you have to stop worrying, wondering, and controlling, and have faith that things will all work out.

Affirm

I no longer allow negative thoughts to drain my energy.
I let go and make room for something better.
All is well, and I notice the good in my life.
Today, I see possibilities and opportunities in my life

January 7

Notice and embrace miracles.

"Be faithful in small things because it is in them that your peace lies."
- Mother Teresa

Today's message

Miracles will start happening for you when you give just as much effort towards your dreams as you do your worries. When we enjoy or focus on the little things in life, the tiny miracles, we notice more of these blessings. Look for the gifts and the miracles (big and small) that happen each and every day for you. Every day may not be good, but there is something good in every day; you just have to look for it. Life is full of beauty, but you will only notice it if you look for it every day. The best part about miracles is that they happen every second of every day; life is a miracle. It becomes your job to notice and seek out the blessings, big and small. Notice and embrace all that life has to offer you today.

Ask yourself

How can I graciously notice the magical blessings from the world around me? What am I most grateful for? Do I notice the abundance around me? How can I change my expectations and appreciate everything?

January 8

Trust you are where you need to be.

*"Stress makes you believe that
everything has to happen right now.
Faith reassures you that everything
will happen in good time."*
- Unknown

Remember

Faith is like taking the first step across a scary bridge when you can't see the other side. Stress and pressure appear when you think you have to figure everything out, but life has a funny way of working out in the end. There is an expression: *if it has not worked out yet, it is not the end.* There is no need to add stress to situations. When you trust that things are unfolding and you are exactly where you need to be, you will feel calmer and more faithful. Thinking this way will allow you to experience more positive emotions and lighten your day!

Affirm

I believe in myself.
I have faith things will work out well for me.
I am patient and trust everything will work out fine.
I am watching as things unfold.
I enjoy the moment that I am in.

January 9

Find your inner power.

*"Smile and let everyone know that today,
you're a lot stronger than you were
yesterday."*
- Drake

Today's message
You are much stronger than you think that you are.
Struggles in your life are developing the strength for
what you need tomorrow and the next day. You are
growing, learning, and experiencing life in a way that
builds your character and resilience. When you feel
like you can't go any further or feel weak and
deflated, just know that you have plenty of power
within you, and the strength that led you this far can
carry you even further. Instead of asking, "Why
me?" ask, "What can I learn from this?" Every day
and every experience will make you more resilient
and capable of growth. Find your inner power today.

Ask yourself
How can I believe in myself a little more? How can I
see the positive, even when I feel like my life is
falling apart? How can I grow and learn from my
experiences? What are my strengths?

January 10

Everything will fall into place.

"Relax. Don't worry.
Everything's going to be alright."
- Old Saying

Remember

Allow your life to unfold as naturally as possible, and trust that everything will fall into place. Sometimes in order to add to your life, you have to subtract something. As humans, we tend to think we need to add to our lives to make them better. But sometimes, you simply need to subtract. Ask yourself: "What can I subtract from my life?" It isn't *who you are* that can hold you back, but rather *who you think you are not* that hinders your life. Start your day looking at what you can remove from your day today? Relax and trust that everything will fall into place today.

Affirm

I appreciate all the good in my life.
I subtract what I need to let go of in my life.
I make space for things to fall into place.
I let go of worry and pressure.
Everything is good and falls into place.

January 11

Open your heart.

*"If there is anything better than
to be loved, it is loving."*
- Anne Frank

Today's message

Take time to show love to the people that are regularly there for you and support you even through tough times. Love is one of those things; the more you give, the better you feel. Be loving towards yourself and other people - you will be surprised by how good it feels. When someone is struggling around you, sometimes the best thing to do is just to listen. It is a true statement that you never honestly know what someone is going through. You could be a little sunshine in what might feel like darkness in their life. When you are struggling, it can be hard to ask for help or even know what help you might be needing. Remember, you are not alone. There are people that want to support you and help you. Take today to open your heart to someone: make a kind, loving gesture or show yourself some care and kindness. Be extra loving today. Open your heart to others and let others open their heart to you.

Ask yourself

How can I be kind and loving to someone in my life today? How can I be loving and kind to others and myself?

January 12

Notice if you're exaggerating fears.

*"If you want to conquer fear,
don't sit home and think about it.
Go out and get busy."*
- Dale Carnegie

Remember

When you despair, you remember all the things that are going wrong or are bad in your life. Reroute your thinking back to hope and positivity. Fear is simply a feeling, a feeling that comes from thoughts, and thoughts can change. When you focus on problems, you will see more problems. You will have more opportunities when you focus on possibilities. Notice where you might be ruminating in worry or fear. Decide to shift this thinking by taking action. One of the best ways to conquer what we fear is to start taking action on it slowly. Be ok with potential failure but keep trying and keep going. Practice, learning, and repetition are the keys to conquering fear. Start small to build your confidence. The only way to get better at something is by doing.

Affirm

I let go of fear and reroute my thinking.
I choose to see opportunity.
I believe in my resources.
My strengths carry me far.

January 13

Take responsibility.

"The moment you take responsibility for everything in your life is the moment you can change anything in your life."
- Hal Elrod

Remember

You sometimes need a great deal of courage to let go of the things or people in your life that no longer serve you well. Your happiness is your responsibility. We don't control our genetics or specific circumstances in our lives, but we do have a great deal of power over our intentional behaviours and thinking. When you take responsibility for your life, you shift the lens to a perspective that is empowering. Take a stand about the things in your life that matter. Ask yourself daily what is important to you, and then find the courage to build it into your life. Who do you want to be? How do you want to show up?

Affirm

I take personal responsibility for my life.
I am courageous.
I take a stand for what is important to me.
I am the budling of the person I want to be and the life I desire for myself.

January 14

Be gentle with yourself and others.

"A kind gesture can reach a wound that only compassion can heal!"
- Dr. Steve Maraboli

Remember

Love and appreciate people around you precisely as they are. Life isn't always easy, and there will be ups and downs. It is essential to be kind and gentle. Practice compassion for both yourself and others. Give yourself and others the gift of unconditional love and acceptance. Halt any tendency to judge or criticize yourself and others. Be gentle with yourself and learn to love and forgive yourself. There is no need to strive for perfection in yourself and others as no one is nor can be perfect. Be your own best friend. As humanity, we are all here to help one another. Think about how you can jump in to help someone today. What help might you be needing? Today, choose to be gentle and kind towards yourself and others.

Affirm

I choose to act with compassion.
I accept myself unconditionally.
I am my own best friend.
I am gentle with myself and others.
I act in loving gentle ways.
I see the good in others.
I see the good in myself.

January 15

Have the willingness to be free.

"Stop letting it bother you; just let it go."
- Old Saying

Today's message
Stop letting things hang over your head that keep bringing you down. When you keep running negative emotions over and over, you will continue to create negative feelings. Be willing to let go of the things that bother you and find the courage to let go of the things you can't change. Know when you need to release old anger and frustration. Shift your focus to another better feeling thought. Hit the proverbial delete button and shift your attention to things and thoughts that make you feel good. Save and give the best part of who you are to the people who deserve to have you in their life. Take responsibility for your happiness. Today, have a willingness to be free from that which brings you down. Choose to stop letting things bother you. Decide to dwell on the things that make you feel good today.

Ask yourself
What can I let go of in my life?
What thoughts bring me joy?
What changes can I make in my life?
What generous and kind people do I welcome into my life?

January 16

Surround yourself with positive
people and situations.

"Surround yourself with positive energy."
- Jackie Mannell

Today's message
One positive thought could override a day that is not
going the way you desired. Stay close to anything
and everything that makes you feel like you are
thrilled to be alive. There are no regrets or reasons
to dwell on negative situations, just learn lessons
and move forward. Surround yourself with the
people that make you feel strong, positive, and
healthy. It is essential to stretch out positive
emotions to enhance our well-being and happiness.
Consider the things in your life that feed you
positively. Choose to surround yourself with
uplifting, positive people and situations today.
Positive emotions feed your well-being and lead to
a more balanced ratio in favour of positivity to
negativity.

Ask yourself
How can I focus on the good that is in my life? How
can I be responsible for the energy that I bring?
What are some fun and positive things I can do?
Who and what brings me positive emotions?

January 17

Set positive intentions.

*"By banishing doubt and trusting your
intuitive feelings, you clear a space for the
power of intention to flow through."*
- Wayne Dyer

Today's message

Set the day's tone by expecting beautiful things to
happen during the day and express gratitude first
thing in the morning. When you wake up, take a
long, deep breath and smile because you are alive.
Worry is a waste of time; good and bad things will
always happen in your life, but if you keep focusing
on the good things and stay positive, you will feel
better. Keep in mind that everyone moves at their
own pace. Live from a place of knowing who you are
and that you don't have to move at the speed of
everyone else. Set intentions to enjoy your day, to
go at your own pace, that you are going to notice
the miracles and blessings within your day, and that
you are grateful for all the opportunities.

Ask yourself

Can I give forgive for yesterday's mistakes and
focus my thoughts positively? What beautiful
things have happened to me lately? How can I
attract good things into my life? What exciting
things might be coming?

January 18

Awaken to your world.

*"The past is your lesson. The present is
your gift. The future is your motivation."*
- Zig Ziglar

Today's message
Concentrate and focus on the world around you and embrace its beauty. Become mindful in the present moment and enjoy the beauty around you. Train your mind to see the positive in every situation, and you will experience your world positively. Start believing today that things are going to change for the better. You have control over what you are looking at and noticing in your life. Awaken to the beauty and the gifts in the present moment. Being present and mindful offers a beautiful opportunity for peace and gratitude. You have exciting, beautiful things coming to you in the future, excellent opportunities for growth and learning from the past as well as in the moment, and you have beauty all around.

Ask yourself
How can I take moments throughout the day to be thoroughly present? What is something important that I can do today? What memory can I make for tomorrow? What would help me awaken to the world?

January 19

You are strong.

*"Put the worst behind you
so the best can find you."*
- Billy Cox

Today's message
Problems and challenges are inevitable in your life. Not one person is immune to struggle. Reaching obstacles could stop you, even knock you down at times, but you can overcome a challenge. Since struggle is inevitable, we can take it as an opportunity to learn, grow, and gain experience. Struggling well is about bouncing back from adversity. Just like when you break a bone, your body repairs the bone but adds extra bone and protection around the fractured area. Trial and suffering can be the fuel to strengthen ambition and inspiration, and help you to achieve great things. Out of struggle can come triumph. How can you tap into your strengths today? Is there some way you can turn past trauma or stress into victory or the perception of triumph?

Ask yourself
How have I overcome difficulties in the past? How can I choose to be a warrior during a challenge? How can I decide to be a hero and not be a victim of the circumstances?

January 20

Reclaim your passion.

"Sometimes life is about risking everything for a dream no one can see but you."
- Unknown

Remember

Allow yourself to be and do all the things you are meant to do and be. What are you passionate about? Who are you when no one is looking? Have you lost your child-like passion for something in your life? When you have a sense of jealousy of someone or someone's else situation, it is a deep longing for what might be missing in your life. Maybe a passion your put on the back burner. You cannot expect others to do what you can do for yourself; take back ownership of your life and regain your self-respect. Follow your passion and you will create a future full of play, purpose, and success. Look at those things you wish you had or wish you were doing yourself and start doing them today.

Affirm

I use my discontent as a message and choose an action that will align with my passion.
I take back my power.
I reclaim the passion inside me.
I am responsible for my life.

January 21

Clear your inner house.

"Sometimes your heart needs more time to accept what your mind already knows."
- Old Saying

Remember

Let your past relationships make you better and not bitter. Sometimes you need to give yourself permission to be hurt, to feel sad, and to be human. Take all the time you need to heal emotionally and release any blocks to healing. Freedom is what you do with what has been done or has happened to you. It is common to be affected by the past. Let go of the people, thoughts, and things that hurt you, but never forget what lessons they taught you. Make time for recovery. What would help you heal? Keep in mind the way out of suffering is in the present moment. You can change your perspective right now in the present moment. Memories can be sticky thoughts; know it does not serve you to repeat them over and over. Healing comes when you let go so that the thoughts and feelings don't negatively impact you now, in the present moment. Change how the past story has affected you, become more like the hero than the victim. What do you need today to nurture your heart?

Affirm

I let go of the hurt and mend my broken heart.

January 22

See the bright side of things.

"When things go wrong,
don't go with them."
- Elvis Presley

Remember

Look beyond imperfections and keep an eye out for opportunities. There is an adage: for every dark cloud; there is a silver lining. Your words and attitude carry incredible power over yourself and others around you. Try to stay in a place of noticing and observing instead of judging and criticizing. When you speak, try to uplift yourself and others. Make a point of seeing the bright side of things and the possibility for growth and learning. Just like a room full of horse poo, there has got to be a beautiful horse around somewhere. Make a conscious effort to look for and seek out the positive in any situation. Instead of focussing on what's wrong, you can focus on what's right. It is not pretending bad things don't happen but choosing to enjoy the good.

Affirm

I see the positive in every situation.
I look for opportunities.
I see the bright side of things.
I focus on what's good.
I choose to look for possible growth.

Live Life Happy

January 23

Love your life.

"Interrupt anxiety with gratitude."
- Danielle Laporte

Today's message

When you notice and love what you have, you will have everything you need at this moment. Get so busy loving your life that you don't have time to worry, fret, or fear. Exercise being grateful and appreciate your life. It is often thought that happiness is something that happens to us. To start loving your life, decide to start thinking of your life more positively. You can't change what happens to you, but you can change how you react to it. Create a happiness diary or journal. Keep adding things you love about your life to this journal each day. Live in the moment and enjoy the present. Try to make sure you are spending most of your time enjoying the present moment. Put something special into today. Brighten up your routines or make a special occasion. Make today count. Spend some time doing what you love today.

Remember

Happiness is a choice, not an end result. Your happiness will only come from you. Some days you just have to create your sunshine.

January 24

Open your mind.

"A mind is like a parachute.
It doesn't work if it isn't open."
- Frank Zappa

Today's message

Compromise is about deciding that the other person has an equal amount of the right to be happy as you do. Life and people are not always perfect, and not everyone will carry the same perspective. Situations will be what you make of them. Relationships will consist of ups and downs, and you are meant to ride through all the challenges while learning and growing. Be open to others' opinions, choices, and values. Recognize that everyone, including yourself, is showing up in diverse ways. Compromise for others and lighten up your views. You do not have to change who you are but rather seek to understand and learn from others. Reframe from fighting for your perspective to be heard. Seek to be open-minded and to understand.

Ask yourself

How can I be more open-minded and curious? How can I broaden my perspective and see myself and others as perfectly imperfect? How can I listen to others to understand their point of view?

January 25

Listen to your inner voice.

"There is a voice that doesn't use words.
Listen."
- Rumi

Today's message

Permit yourself to walk away from anything that gives you a bad feeling. Your inner voice needs hearing when it speaks. Listen to positive people and ignore the negative people that doubt, judge, or criticize. Deeper to that, listen to that inner voice and nudge that is deep inside you. Get quiet in your mind and silence the chaos or noise from the world so you can hear your inner voice. It's ok to have negative thoughts; just don't let negative thinking take control. Pump up the volume on your intuition and your inner voice. Pay attention to your emotions and set intentions to tune into your inner voice. When your mind takes over, take a moment to pause, breathe into it, and create space for your inner voice to come through. Listen to what your gut is telling you today!

Ask yourself

Do other people's opinions drown out my inner voice? A voice inside me is whispering to me all day long: what is it saying? How can I pay attention to my inner voice and avoid overriding what it's saying? What is my inner voice telling me?

January 26

Relax and take a deep breath.

"If you want to be happy,
you have to be happy on purpose."
- Joel Osteen

Today's message

Sometimes, it's hard to pick right from wrong. The best thing you can do is go with all your heart, take a deep breath, and hope it all goes well. You may not be ok right now, but it will all be ok. Stopping and taking a deep breath can help calm you and reconnect you to the present moment. Soon, when you look back on challenging periods in your life, you are going to be so glad you never gave up. Connect to your breath in times of trial, and even when you are not going through a challenge, when you simply want an energy boost or restoration of your spirit. Stop, breathe, and relax. Be happy on purpose today because you decided to be happy!

Affirm

All is well, and I am ok.
I am going to make it.
My breath feeds my soul.
I let go of stress with my breath.
I inhale life and exhale all that I don't need.
I stop and take a deep breath.
My breath nourishes my body and calms my mind.

January 27

Have some fun.

"Find some beautiful place to get lost."
- Elliott Smith

Remember

You can't always play it safe. If a sailboat stayed in the safe harbour, it would never see the beautiful sea. Get out and have fun, find joy and lose track of time. In the end, you will only regret the chances and opportunities that you didn't take. Life is about having fun and enjoying yourself. Take risks and fully experience your life. Don't be afraid of experience, because the more knowledge you gain, the more energy, happiness, and love you will have. Try new ways to have fun; have a dance party, smile at someone, finger paint, do something random, be spontaneous, look up at the clouds, skip instead of walk, try a new recipe, plant a garden, play a game, ride a bike, dance in the rain. Try to infuse more moments of play into your day, lose track of time and let your inner child come out. What fun thing can you add to today?

Affirm

I am trying something new.
I am awake and alive.
I get lost in my experiences.
I seek out opportunities to play and have fun.

January 28

Do what brings you comfort.

"Set peace of mind as your highest goal and organize your life around it."
- Brian Tracy

Today's message

Think about the things that make you feel good. What has helped you to feel comfortable in the past? Try to make a list of all the things you enjoy so that you can draw on this list when you require comfort. Whether it's a nice bath, a walk-in nature, or simply reading a good book, you will know what to do when you need peace and comfort. Awareness of what brings you comfort is essential in times of struggle. Think about and make a list of the things that bring support to your heart. Do you need comfort today? It is fun to make joy your magnet for the day. What brings you joy, and how can you attract these things into your life, or do you need to go out and do?

Ask yourself

What warms my heart? What activities make me feel good? When I need comforting, who can I talk to? What would optimize my life around me? How can I bring more comfort into my life?

January 29

Connect to your playful self.

"Can your inner child come out and play?"
- David Icke

Today's message

You are meant to enjoy life and do the things that please you. Go out with your friends, or plan something different than you would typically do. It does not matter how old you are; there is an inner child within you that seeks fun and laughter. Playfulness leads to creative thinking and decision-making. Play offers the chance to experience more positive emotions like happiness and joy. Just because you are an adult doesn't mean you can't play. Play is a mood booster. Re-evaluate how you spend your time. Enjoy quality time with your family and friends. How can you be silly? Consider what your quirks are and how you were silly as a child. Bring out more play in your life. Find reasons to laugh and be extra crazy today. Exaggerate your quirkiness.

Ask yourself

How can I love and nurture the part of me that is my inner child? What child-like wonder can I surround myself with? How can I look at the world with child-like fearlessness? What would be fun to do? How can I be silly and funny?

January 30

Enjoy the moment.

*"Life is a gift. Never forget to enjoy and
bask in every moment you are in."*
- Celestine Chua

Remember
Turn inward and learn from your inner voice, and you will see the world more clearly. Being mindful allows magic to flow into your life. In each moment, you receive clues and gifts that guide you for your future. Enjoy the moments today! Pay attention to your senses to help bring you into the present moment. What are you seeing, feeling, smelling, tasting, touching, hearing? Being grateful or practicing gratitude in the moment is a beautiful way to be more present. Mindfulness quiets the typical monkey mind and allows for peace. When you are mindful, you activate the logical portion of your brain and calm the brain's stress center.

Affirm
I celebrate my life and enjoy this moment.
I train my brain to see and appreciate the world around me.
I see clearly, and I am present in the moment.
I enjoy all the gifts here in the present moment.

January 31

Leave behind what isn't serving you.

*"Stop focusing on how stressed you are
and remember how blessed you are."*
- Gautama Buddha

Today's message
Every trial and challenge in life has a hidden blessing or gift. Let go or leave behind the things in life that are not positively serving you. Shift your perspective from a place of stress to a place of gratitude. Suppose you don't like something - welcome positive change. Challenges can bring about new opportunities full of growth and learning. Take with you the chance to grow and let go of thoughts weighing you down or holding you back. It is easy to worry, ruminate, or dwell on stressful situations, but this only makes you feel bad. Take the opportunity to shift to focusing on finding hidden blessings, the potential for learning, and opportunities for growth.

Ask yourself
What part of my life is turned upside down? What is another way to see this? What would happen if I looked at things differently and welcomed positive change? How can I let go of the things that are not helping me to flourish?

February 1

A new beginning.

"Every day is a new beginning;
take a deep breath and start again."
- Ritu Ghatourey

Today's message

Approach life as if it is a continual stream of new beginnings. Make space in your life for new beautiful things to arrive. Enjoy the idea of starting something new or the birth of good things. The joy of life comes from new opportunities and experiences. Keep growing and changing. Let go of old items that don't serve you any longer. Release clutter from your mind, space, and life that no longer have much life left in them. Be open to new beginnings. Starting something new brings new opportunities, and it can be empowering. You will probably learn new lessons while learning and growing. That new beginning might just be the start of something exciting and life changing.

Ask yourself

What can I release that is worn or old? What needs refreshing in my life? How can I stretch my mind today? What new things could come my way?

February 2

Avoid thinking about
what you don't want.

*"Watch your thoughts, they become
words. Watch your words; they become
actions. Watch your actions; they become
habits."*
- Winston Churchill

Today's message

Be careful how you think because your thoughts are potent. Thoughts end up making you feel a certain way, and then that becomes your reality. What you think about, and your perspective is much more meaningful and important than. Often the focus is placed on the things you do not desire, but little emphasis is placed on thinking about what you do desire for yourself. Use the power of your mind to manifest what you desire for yourself in your life when you become a form of your visualization, dreaming, and manifestation. Take time to think about what you do want in your life. Halt the thoughts of what you don't like or desire. You can mentally prepare for the life you want for yourself.

Ask yourself

How can I use my mind to focus on what I desire? If I allow myself to dream, what is my ideal life, and what action can I take every day?

February 3

Everything has perfect timing.

"Take life day by day and be grateful for the little things. Don't get stressed over what you can't control."
- Unknown

Remember

Be in love with your life and the loving people that you already have in it. It's during this time life feels so much brighter. If you keep moving forward while taking notice of the gifts around you, everything will come to you at the right time. When you adopt this trusting flow frame of mind, you let go of scarcity and lack, and make room for everything to show up and unfold as it should. That is not to say stop taking action and showing up in your life, but instead release the pressure and stress around timing. Trust that everything will show up at the perfect time. Enjoy the moments you are in today.

Affirm

I have faith all will work out well.
I appreciate the love and support around me.
Good things are unfolding in my life.
I take things day by day.

February 4

Remain positive and keep dreaming.

"Stay positive even when it feels like your whole world is falling apart."
- Old Saying

Today's message

Keep your head up and stay positive. The tough challenges you face will help you grow and learn. Challenge and struggle are a part of being human. When you find yourself in disruption, choose a growth mindset. No matter how much things can hurt in certain situations, one day, you will look back on challenges and realize those times have changed your life for the better. Good things will come to you, and you will feel better amongst challenges when you believe that better things are coming, that there is potential for growth and learning, as well as perhaps a new direction for you.

Ask yourself

How can I stay positive, work harder, and make things happen? How can I shift my focus to what matters and makes me feel good? Although times might be challenging, how can I keep moving forward?

February 5

Take a break from negativity.

"The less you respond to negative people,
the more peaceful your life will become."
- Unknown

Remember

When you are positive and grateful, you send out good energy, and beautiful things will be attracted into your life. When you focus on the things that bring you positive emotions, your world feels much better. The opposite is also true. Whatever is bringing you down - people, thoughts, or situations - try to get rid of it as fast as possible, so you don't have as much negativity in your life. Never underestimate the power of a positive explanatory style of thinking and acting. We become what we think about most of the time.

Affirm

Today, I choose to focus on good things.
Negative energy is not welcome here.
I think positively and abundantly.
I choose to focus on things that make me feel positive emotions.
I minimize talking about things that don't make me feel good.

February 6

Nurture your dreams.

"Have patience.
Everything is difficult before it is easy."
- Saadi Shirazi

Today's message

Have faith that the seeds you have planted and your life will start to grow. Everything in life that is worth having takes time, nurturing, and care to expand. When you look at someone who has achieved their dreams, or you have a mentor you look up to, what you don't always see is the hard work, determination, and consistent effort that has been put into accomplishing their success. When something is not working for you, be patient and trust that it will work if it is supposed to. Give your dreams a chance to grow! Don't give up too quickly if things are not working as desired. But also, evaluate when it is time to let things go.

Ask yourself

What can I nurture in my life? How can I step back and allow each moment to bring joy? When can I take time for my development? Where do I need to let off pressure?

February 7

Release.

*"Saying yes to happiness means learning
to say no to the things and people that
stress you out."*
- Thema Davis

Today's message
There are going to be things and people in your life
that do not feel good. It is essential to let go of
situations that are out of your control. Also, choose
the quality of people you spend your time with. Let
joy be your magnet; in other words, go to the
things that bring you happiness and joy. Move
away from or release the things that cause you
discontent or stress. Take a good hard look at your
life; what and who brings you to joy? Determine
the things that are no longer bringing you joy, and
if you can eliminate or decrease exposure. Take
time to run through your day and notice the
thoughts, people, or situations that need releasing
or minimizing.

Ask yourself
Who in my life brings me a sense of peace and
support? What needs to be minimized? What can I
let go of?

February 8

Have faith in yourself.

*"Your faith can move mountains,
and your doubt can create them."*
- Old Saying

Today's message

Faith is about believing you don't know what will happen in your life, but you know that things will happen, and it will all work out fine. You can't control everything that happens in your life, and you can't control the future, but you can relax and have faith that all things will work out. There may be challenging circumstances in your life; faith is about trusting in your ability to handle what life has to throw at you, and that you will come out the other side just fine. If you believe in yourself and your abilities, anything is possible for you. Shift your perspective to one that believes you are the driver of your success and happiness. Let go of any limiting beliefs that might be holding you back from having faith in yourself.

Ask yourself

Where do I lack faith? What challenges have I had in my life that have led to beautiful outcomes? What dreams do I want to follow? How can I believe in myself a little more?

February 9

Find the power within.

"Beautiful things happen in your life
when you distance yourself
from the negative things."
- Zig Ziglar

Remember

Strength shows up in your ability to persist and continue even amongst challenges. Never underestimate your power to change yourself and bring about more inner strength. Strength and growth come from continual exposure to effort, persistence, and challenge. What are your strengths or superpowers? What would a best friend say about you? What would someone who loves you say your strengths are? Start to journal a list of your strengths and how you have used your strengths to help you in your life. Inner strength is like a muscle. The more you train it, the stronger it becomes. Put yourself first to build your power and train your mind and body to make it stronger. Decide on things you want for yourself, commit to them, and then take action.

Affirm

My inner power is beautiful.
I am strong and powerful.
I use my strengths as often as I can.
I focus on my strengths.

February 10

Move into gratitude and
appreciation.

*"The happiest people don't have
the best of everything; they just make
the best of everything."*
- Unknown

Today's message
Gratitude and appreciation put you into a place of
positivity. The positive emotions that come with
appreciation and gratitude are powerful. It is a
beautiful positive intervention to move you to a
better feeling state. Sometimes we try to rush or
force life and focus on lack. Moving into being
grateful for what is already eases pressure.
Eventually, all the pieces of your life puzzle will fall
into place. Trust that all the details will reveal
themselves at the perfect time. Keep yourself
occupied with positive thoughts and gratitude.
Practicing gratitude has incredible effects. Explore
ways you can be more appreciative. Observe, decide
to be thankful today, and affirm all the good things.

Ask yourself
What am I most grateful for today? What am I
appreciative of today? How can I show expressions
of gratitude to others? What do I appreciate about
myself right now?

February 11

Move on and start fresh.

"As you waste your energy complaining about life, someone out there is struggling to breathe. Appreciate what you have. Be thankful and stop complaining."
- Unknown

"Every day is a fresh start."
- Dagny Scott Barrios

Today's message

Shift your focus from focusing on problems or challenges to concentrate on things you are grateful for in your life. If you catch yourself dwelling on problems, make a mental switch towards appreciation of what is good. Sometimes the best action to take is simply to start fresh. Every day you have a chance to learn and grow from experiences. Seize the opportunity to learn and expect great things to come. It is a new day! Be open to seeing possibilities, being courageous, and being grateful.

Affirm

I am grateful for the good in my life.
My life is full of gifts.
I put my energy into appreciating life.

February 12

Release worry and fear.

*"When you expect the best, you release
a magnetic force in your mind which,
by the law of attraction,
tends to bring the best to you."*
- Norman Vincent Peale

Today's message

Hope for the best. Begin to expect only good things coming to you from any situation. You can conquer fear, but you have to make up your mind to do so. Negative, fearful thoughts can destroy you; change your thinking towards noticing more positive. It is common to worry and ruminate about things that could go wrong. You might even go down the path of "what if" thinking. Shift your thinking from focusing on problems or challenges to focusing on things you are grateful for in your life. You can shift your thinking just like changing the channel on your tv.

Ask yourself

How can I take my mind off any troubles and get my mind to focus on my needs? What am I worrying about typically? When I am on the worry channel, what channel do I want to change to? Love channel? Joy channel? Nature channel?

February 13

Be mindful and seek value.

"Sometimes you will never know the true value of a moment until it becomes a memory."
- Dr. Seuss

Today's message
Even when things seem dark or terrible, the darkness will end and give way to brightness and good. Sometimes having things not go the way you want is a beautiful stroke of luck. Express emotions and let go of the hurt. There is power in finding the beauty in the challenging things that happen to you. In the moment, the things that happen might not seem valuable. Take time to be present in the moment and mindful of the hidden gifts. Take time to appreciate the moment you are in and value the people and situations. To encourage mindfulness, slow down, meditate, focus on one thing at a time, eat mindfully, have check-in times, or spend time in nature.

Ask yourself
Maybe it is not a good day today, but how is it alright? What learning is inside my pain and disappointment? How can I be mindful and appreciate the value of each day? What are the hidden gifts today?

February 14

It's time to unburden your pain.

"When someone treats you like crap, just remember it's because there's something wrong with them, not you."
- Karen Salmansohn

Remember

Sadness is only a temporary experience, and it will pass. Be ok with your uneasiness, as it is a sign that you are human. There is a message in negative emotions such as pain, disappointment, anger, and frustration. Look at these emotions and process the potential message. Choose to see your challenges as hidden blessings and expect good things to come from difficult situations. The past is where you learn your lessons; you can use them and apply them in the future. Keep in mind the pain you feel might result from someone else's issues, not yours. Don't take it personally and see what opportunities might lie in the message of your emotions.

Affirm

I am ready to grow and learn.
I let go of past hurt and pain.
I honour my emotions as messages.
I acknowledge my sadness and focus forward.

February 15

Nourish and blossom.

"Every beautiful butterfly was once a dreary caterpillar."
- Old Saying

Remember

Each day is an opportunity to blossom and emerge into your beautiful life. Change is a process of growing into the special person you were meant to be. Take time to grow, learn, and evolve. If you get better and you see success as a result, use that as motivation to keep getting better. How can you learn and grow more today? What would nourish you on a deep level? Is there something you've wanted to try or do that would feel great if you did it today? What makes you blossom? Just like a flower needs sunshine to blossom, humans need love to flourish. How do you act in loving ways? You are a social animal; you cannot exist without others. Seek out the love and support of family, friends, and associates to help nourish you.

Affirm

I am getting better every day.
Things are emerging for me.
I nourish myself and grow every day.
I enjoy learning and trying new things.
I spread love and receive love.
I nourish my soul with others.

February 16

Listen to your intuition.

"Once you make a decision, the universe conspires to make it happen."
- Ralph Waldo Emerson

Today's message

Make a decision and don't look back. Sometimes it is the minor decisions that can change your life. When you are clear on your goals, dreams, and desires for yourself, it becomes easier to move forward into your day. By listening deeply to yourself and your inner voice, you will clarify what you desire for yourself. It is time to take charge. Don't base your decision on other people's advice, they do not have to deal with the consequence of the decision. This is your life; turn down the volume on the input of others and formulate your own decisions. You can welcome perspective, but ultimately, listen to your intuition and make your own consequential decisions.

Ask yourself

What is my intuition saying to me? I am in control: how can I take charge of my own life? What decisions do I need to make? What do I desire for myself?

February 17

Notice the treasures in your life.

"If you look the right way, you can see the whole world is a garden."
- Frances Hodgson Burnett

Today's message

Embrace your life and count your blessings. Own your own story and love yourself through the process. All your needs are continuously met, and anything is possible for you. Lack exists in your mind. Raise your standards for your life and your needs will be met. Appreciate what you already have and watch your prosperity and wealth increase. Sometimes all you need to do is take a deep cleansing breath. Pick yourself up, look around, and trust that everything is happening the way it is supposed to for you. Can you think of any hidden blessings in your life? What gifts are surrounding you?

Ask yourself

How can I embrace who I am and not apologize for being me? Can I see prosperity in my life? What gifts are surrounding me now? Where are my opportunities, ideas, and support?

February 18

Big transformations revitalize you.

*"Don't be afraid of change because it is
leading you to a new beginning."*
- Joyce Meyer

Today's message

Change can seem scary if you focus on what you
have to give up, but change is exciting when you
think about what you will gain. Decide to transform
in some way today. When things are not going well
in your life, find a new path that will lead you in a
new direction. Change over time in your life is
inevitable, but your transformation is a personal
choice. Give birth to something new in your life. It
takes courage to show up for your life and try
something new. There is a spark inside you. You just
have to fire it up and let that spark shine.

Ask yourself

What is most important to me? How can I build my
life around what is important to me? What would I
do if I put myself on the top of my to-do list today?
Is it time to start something new and have a new
beginning?

February 19

Be careful with your thinking.

"Whatever you believe about yourself on the inside is what you will manifest on the outside."
- Mahatma Gandhi

Remember

Pay close attention to your thinking today. Notice the inner critic or negative voice taking over. Finding the inner critic is sometimes hard as it becomes automatic. Listen closely when you are mean to yourself. What we repeat over and over become strong messages. Rethink your thinking. Take notice of your thinking and hit the PAUSE or DELETE button on those thoughts. You can also turn them down or simply talk back to those thoughts. The inner critic is often trying to keep you safe. You can listen to the inner critic, so it feels heard and then let it know, you will be safe. Pay more attention to what you allow to enter your mind and how it is influencing your life. Be careful with your words as they heavily influence your actions.

Affirm

Today, I am careful with my thinking.
I train my inner critic not to be as loud.
I welcome my thoughts, and I work with them.

February 20

Love yourself more.

"What if you simply devoted this day to loving yourself more?"
- Unknown

Remember

Try and remember the things that make you happy. It is incredible how fast you forget to show yourself careful, loving attention in this busy world. Self-compassion, self-care, and self-love are essential to your well-being. What makes you happy that you could add to your day? How can you love yourself more? Simply by taking the time to give yourself some kindness, you open the door to a beautiful day. Being kind and loving yourself more might feel strange at first, but it is essential to self-compassion and self-care. To love yourself more, you can move more often, eat healthy, limit things that aren't good for you, get plenty of sleep, add play to your life, and make time for rest and relaxation. You show you are a loveable person by honouring what brings you joy! Treat yourself well today.

Ask yourself

What makes me feel good? What makes me feel loved? How can I love myself more today?

February 21

Run your race.

*"Take the risk of thinking for yourself.
Much more happiness, truth, beauty, and
wisdom will come to you that way."*
- Christopher Hitchens

Today's message
Everyone has their own lane, maintain yours and
you will notice it feels more comfortable to focus on
yourself. When you are constantly thinking of and
worried about what others are thinking, saying, or
feeling, you end up trying to please people. It is
important to think about your feelings, needs, and
perspective first. There is peace and strength that
come from believing in yourself and all that you are.
Know that you are important. A flower does not
compete with the flower next to it, because they all
bloom and are uniquely beautiful. Use others as
inspiration for your unique mission. Don't let it bring
you down.

Ask yourself
How can I stay focused on my own life? What
makes me powerful? How can I just do me? What
does my lane look like?

February 22

Have the willingness to be free and allow yourself to emerge.

"Stop letting it bother you. Just let it go."
- Old Saying

Today's message

Stop letting things hang over you that keep bringing you down. Be willing to let go of the things that bother you and find the courage to let go of the things you can't change. Know when you need to release old anger and frustration. Save and give the best part of who you are to the people who deserve to have it in their life. Now and then you need to shed what isn't serving you. Shake off the deadwood. When you let go, there is a new you that emerges. It is still made up of you at the core but a bright, fresh, and renewed version of you. You have reinvented a better understanding of yourself that is not afraid, has personal boundaries, and sprouts firmly out into the world. You are getting better, stronger, and wiser every day.

Ask yourself

What do I need to let go of in my life? What changes can I make in my life? What generous and kind people can I welcome into my life? What do I desire for myself?

February 23

Learning opportunity.

*"Failure is only the opportunity to begin
again, only this time more wisely."*
- Henry Ford

Remember

Don't be too hard on yourself. Look at everything as an opportunity to learn something new. Just when your world seems crazy and stressful, beautiful things will happen. It's hard to know and find strength when you are amid a challenge or a stormy situation, but one step at a time, one breath at a time, you will get through this. Learn from your experiences and use them positively. Hold on tight. As Barbara Haines Howett put it, *"Just when the caterpillar thought the world was ending, she became a butterfly."* See if you can find the benefits in all things. If you can spot or discover the potential learning opportunity, you will turn pain into purpose and struggle. Throughout your day seek out learning opportunities.

Ask yourself

What lessons have I learned? What can I take away from this? How do I explain this to myself?

February 24

You have what you need within.

*"Everything will be ok in the end,
and if it's not ok, it not the end."*
- Old Saying

*"Life has many ways of testing a person's
will, either by having nothing happen at all
or by having everything happen all at
once."*
- Paulo Coelho

Today's message

Everything will be good soon. Just hang in there and don't worry yourself about it too much. Tough times don't last. Look for things you can appreciate and be grateful for what is around you today to shift your energy. Vision is the ability to see potential in what others overlook. A true tragedy in your life would be to let your talent die inside you. Awaken to your potential today. Only put blinders on to block those things that conspire to hold you back. See that all that you need is within you.

Affirm

Today is a new day. I am ok.
It's ok to be just ok.
I look for magic in my daily routine.
I wake up to my life. I am full of potential.

February 25

Look at your routines.

"To change your life, you need to change your priorities."
- John C. Maxwell

Today's message

To establish what takes priority in your life, you must be willing to say no to something else. Take time to step back and examine what's important to you in life. Make that your priority. When you let go, you are making space and room for something even bigger and better. Take time to do fun things. Sometimes we need to step out of work and responsibility and into the role of fun and recreation. It's ok to make time for yourself and have fun. This will help balance your life and make you feel happier. Look at all areas of your life and make sure you are making time to waste time simply. Don't feel guilty for doing fun things for yourself.

Ask yourself

What are my priorities? Can I remove commitments that do not bring me happiness? What needs my attention now? What would make me feel more balanced? What can I do that is simply fun for me? What time wasters fill me up with happiness? What makes me feel energized?

February 26

Claim your power.

"BElieve in YOUrself."
- Expression

Today's message
You have within you right now everything you need to deal with whatever the world may throw at you. Having a low opinion of yourself is not "modesty." It's self-destructive. Hold who you are in high regard. Shift your perspective to being in control instead of being controlled. The most common way that someone loses their power is that they think they don't have any. Distance yourself from the world and connect again with your voice. Claim your power today.

Ask yourself
How can I take responsibility for my life? What are my unique gifts and talents? How can I flex the muscle of courage?

Affirm
I am strong and hold myself in high regard.
I have all that I need within me to deal with a challenge.
I believe in myself.
I am enough.

February 27

Set positive intentions.

"Wake up, smile, and tell yourself:
'Today is my day.'"
- Old Saying

Today's message
Problems and challenges are inevitable in your life. Reaching obstacles *could* stop you, but the worst is behind you, and you *are* capable of overcoming challenges. Trial and suffering can be the fuel to strengthen ambition and inspiration and can help you achieve great things. Set the tone for the day by expecting beautiful things to happen during the day. Set yourself up with positive intentions by creating mantras or statements you can repeat to yourself. Create rituals or share your choices with others. Ask for what you want, then get it. Express gratitude first thing in the morning when you wake up, take a long deep breath and smile because you are alive. Worry is a waste of time. Good and bad things will always happen in your life, but you just have to keep focusing on the good things and stay positive.

Ask yourself
Can I give forgiveness for yesterday's mistakes and focus on positive thoughts? What good intentions do I have for today? What mantra or saying would help me?

February 28

Find your happy place.

"Anything that gets your blood racing is probably worth doing."
- Hunter Thompson

Today's message

When you have great passion, you can make anything happen. Discover YOU and find your passion and life purpose. What do you value? What makes you excited? What brings you a sense of meaning? Your passion will eventually lead you to your purpose. Whatever your mind can think of, dream of, or conceive, you can achieve. Get clues from the things that excite you! Finding the things that bring you positive emotions like joy, excitement, and pleasure is key to your well-being. What brings you excitement? What used to bring you excitement as a child? Everyone has a place where they feel safe and happy. It can be a physical place to visit or an imagined place. Find your happy place that will be a respite that recharges you. Recall places that you enjoy the sounds, visuals. Where have you felt content and stayed open-minded?

Ask yourself

What excites me and makes me feel enthusiastic? What is important? What is my burning desire? What would I be doing if there were no obstacles? Who am I when no one is watching?

February 29
(Bonus/Leap Year)

Be optimistic and stay determined.

"Optimism is a happiness magnet.
If you stay positive, good things and good
people will be drawn to you."
- Mary Lou Retton

Remember
Keep going so you can be successful; make mistakes, but don't quit. Try not to concern yourself with when your time will come, rather keep growing, learning, and preparing for a great future. Never stop believing in yourself and maintain hope because miracles happen every single day. Be optimistic about your future and stay determined to reach what you desire. Every day is hopeful about your future and keeps moving closer and closer towards the future you dream of achieving.

Affirm
I am patient and expect great things to come.
I visualize my dreams.
I stay determined and optimistic.

March 1

It will be ok.

"Let every moment be what it's going to be. What's meant to be will come your way. What's not will fall away. Relax, don't worry."
- Mandy Hale

Remember

The truth is that you will not always be ok and that times will be tough. The good news is that everything will be ok. When you feel weak, you need to honour how you feel and stay strong because everything will be ok. Offer yourself compassion and be your own best friend when you are down because that is a very important message you are telling yourself. Further to that, tell yourself it will be ok and believe it! Offer yourself care and acknowledge this is tough, and that you will be ok. Permit yourself to be human. You are strong, and it is not weak to have emotions and to feel strain through struggle. Know that in the end, it will be ok.

Affirm

I take comfort in knowing things will be ok.
I know I will be ok.
I support myself and heal.
I offer comfort to myself in times of challenge.

March 2

Find a calm environment.

"You can't calm the storm, so stop trying.
What you can do is calm yourself.
The storm will pass."
- Timber Hawkeye

Today's message

Sometimes you need to surround yourself with gentle people for the sake of having a soft place to fall, like how a teddy bear or soft pillow feels comforting. Calm, soothing, and peaceful environments are crucial to your well-being. Keep your sweetness and detach yourself from any bitterness in your world. A calm environment can bring inner strength and confidence. Surround yourself with people and things that have a calming effect on you. Today, play calm music, speak peacefully, soothe yourself in a bath, meditate, or take deep breaths.

Ask yourself

How can I be gentle with myself? What needs to happen to be kind to myself and others? How can I choose and direct my thinking to a peaceful place?

March 3

Be clear on your intentions.

"When your intentions are very pure and clear, nature brings support to you."
- Sri Sri Ravi Shankar

Today's message

When you are crystal clear on your intentions and desires, you will be amazed at what will show up for you in your life. When you become clear on your intentions, you will be more inspired to take action. Do everything with a good heart and positive intentions, and in return you will never be disappointed. Listen to your voice and nudges instead of the loud noise in the world. You have instincts built right into you. Trust the inner alarm bells, enthusiastic excitement, and inner voice. Listen to others that offer support and leave the decision up to you. Trust yourself to make good decisions and get clear on your intentions.

Ask yourself

What is the 'why' behind everything I do? Am I living from habit or living more from intention? What are my intentions?

March 4

Notice dissatisfaction
and let it motivate you.

*"One's best success comes after their
greatest disappointments."*
- Henry Ward Beecher

Remember

The feeling of being stuck is painful, but this feeling of struggle can encourage positive change and growth. Things will change in your life in direct proportion to the disappointment you feel; embrace that feeling of discontent as motivation to make things happen. The only person you have to blame for feeling disappointed is you. Blame yourself for not fulfilling your dreams. Undertake new projects and remember your dreams. Honestly admit problems. Accept and face the things you need to conquer. When you find the courage to admit you may have a problem, you then have the power to get over it and grow. Sometimes we need to acknowledge our fears, addictions, or excuses so that we can face them straight on and get through them.

Affirm

I use negative feelings as motivation for change.
I embrace the discontent in my life.
I follow my truth and look for new experiences.

March 5

Release negative thoughts
and keep your head up.

"Don't worry about a thing.
Every little thing is going to be alright."
- Bob Marley

Today's message

Life is a balance between what you can control and what you cannot. Let go of the things you cannot control. Manage what you expect in your life, limit your need to control, and peace will come. Let go of negative thoughts and things in your life and replace them with good things and thoughts. Train your mind to see the good in every single situation and person. Being positive in a negative situation is a tough but essential decision you can make. Sometimes good things in your life have to fall apart and crumble to come together for new opportunities. Ask yourself: How can I let life's events come freely and welcome all lessons? What am I trying to control in my life?

Affirm

I am staying strong, and I focus on the good things.
I see the positive in adverse situations.
I keep my head up.

March 6

Remain positive and keep dreaming.

*"Welcome the challenges. Look for the
opportunities in every situation
to learn and grow in wisdom."*
- Brian Tracy

Today's message
Keep your head up and stay positive. The tough
challenges you face will help you grow and learn. No
matter how much things can hurt in current
situations, one day you will look back on challenges
and realize those times have changed your life for
the better. Good things will come to you when you
believe that better things are coming. No one is
immune to the ups and downs of life, so when you
are in the downtimes look for the good and the
possibilities that might be birthed out of this
struggle. You just have to keep looking for the
miracles and blessings.

Ask yourself
How can I stay positive, work harder and make
things happen? How can I shift my focus to what
matters and brings on good emotions? Good things
happen when you least expect them; how can I
keep moving forward?

March 7

Notice abundance all around you.

"Don't wait for everything to be perfect before you decide to enjoy your life."
- Joyce Meyer

Remember

Miracles happen every single day. The problem is you forget to notice them. Laugh, be grateful, breathe deep, appreciate, hug, and dream big. Make wishes and watch them come true! Refine what it is that you expect in life; stop hoping and start acting on your dreams. Focusing on what you do have instead of what you do not have will move you from scarcity thinking to abundant thinking. Take notice of all the abundance all around you today. Put a timer on and take note of the abundance around you throughout your day.

Affirm

I notice all the miracles in my life.
I pay attention and notice abundance all around me.
I properly manage my expectations.
I see all the abundance in my life.

March 8

Respect yourself.

***"How you treat yourself is how you are
inviting the world to treat you."***
- Unknown

Today's message

How you treat yourself sets the standard for how you would like the world to treat you. You have control over how you treat yourself. Choose to be kind to yourself, eat well, get plenty of sleep, and exercise. Love yourself enough to set your boundaries. Setting up your rights will help you set boundaries. Boundaries are like fences. They keep you safe in your backyard. Your time, your energy, and your life are all about your own boundaries that you set. Drawing a line in the sand and stating your boundaries is a form of self-respect and honouring your own needs. You are worthy of good treatment. Decide today to treat yourself with respect and honour.

Affirm

I treat myself with respect.
I make good choices for myself.
I set healthy boundaries.
I state my values and rights.

March 9

Awaken the power within you.

"Your mind is a powerful thing.
When you fill it with positive thoughts,
your life will start to change."
- Gautama Buddha

Today's message

Tap into the power that you have inside you. Find peace in knowing that everyone has a super-power and unique gift. Make time to focus on what makes you powerful. Choose to take notice of your positive attributes. Believe in yourself because you are more powerful than you may realize. Avoid the nay-sayers and non-believers. You are powerful when you know that you can do anything and keep focusing on your greatness. Look inside, that is where your inner strength lies, not outside of yourself. Ask yourself: Am I pulled in the direction of haters? How can I think of the special people that love me? Life can be challenging; how can I go out and be powerful?

Affirm

I am powerful.
I have special gifts that support me.
I focus on my positive traits.

March 10

Avoid being self-critical
or judgmental.

*"One small positive thought in the morning
can change your whole day."*
- Dalai Lama

Today's message

Try to be your own best friend. Consider how you talk to yourself in your mind. Is it nice? Is it encouraging? Start your day by focusing on your strengths and what you have to bring to this exciting new day. Stop or delete negative, self-critical, or judgmental thoughts about yourself. Re-write your thinking by building up your strengths and being nice to yourself. Go on a negative diet. When you are positive and grateful, you send out good energy and beautiful things to your life. Whatever is bringing you down, try to get rid of it as fast as possible, so you don't have negativity in your life. Never underestimate the power of positive emotions and acting in positive kind ways, even towards yourself.

Affirm

I am my own best friend.
I delete or cancel negative statements about myself.
I speak loving, kind words about myself.

March 11

See the world in a fresh way.

"Dear Stress, I'm breaking up with you."
- Ky-Lee Hanson

Remember Life isn't about waiting for an opportunity to come to you. Instead, you need to get out there and try new adventures for yourself. Release the need to fight the old and welcome the new into your life. Release worry and fear. Hope for the best and begin to expect only good things coming to you from any situation. You can face any fear, but you have to make up your mind to do so. Negative thoughts can destroy you; change your thinking to positive. Ask yourself: Can I take my mind off troubles and get my mind to focus on my needs? When has my thinking been negative? Can I look for the positive and opportunities for growth in everything?

Affirm
I feel new beginnings coming to me.
I see the world with fresh eyes. Positive changes are coming my way.
I have the power to change the channel of my thoughts.

March 12

Reroute your attention.

"You can't start the next chapter of your life if you keep re-reading the last one."
- Unknown

Today's message

If a bad mood has you in its grip, remember it is better to have hope and think optimistically than to despair. Choose to chase your dreams instead of deciding to run from your fears. Dwell on what is going fantastic and what is working, not on what is going wrong. Acknowledge and learn from what is not working, but then reroute your attention to possibilities. Avoid dwelling on problems and focus on solutions or opportunities. Everything can be seen as either an opportunity to learn and grow or an obstacle that keeps you stuck. You get to choose.

Ask yourself

How can I talk to myself? What is working in my life? What's good? What would hitting the reset button look like? What would it look like if I push through fear and doubt?

March 13

Embrace life with excitement.

"Enthusiasm is the sparkle in your eyes, the swing in your step, the grip in your hand, the irresistible surge of will and energy to execute your ideas."
- Henry Ford

Remember

An enthusiastic heart finds opportunities everywhere. Stop worrying about what can go wrong and get super excited about what can go right. One of the best ways to get what you want and find enthusiasm in life is to be grateful for what you already have. Don't be satisfied with mediocrity. You were made for great things. Expect more from yourself than from others because expectations will keep you aspiring for more. Keep your excitement alive. Demand more from yourself, and you never know what you can do. Know your worth and never settle for less than you deserve. Make no apologies for high standards. Follow your excitement in life. It can never steer you wrong. Ask yourself: What's exciting today? How can I build my excitement level?

Affirm

Today, I am excited about everything.
I am excited about all the good things to come.
I am grateful for my life.

March 14

Take notice of the beauty
in your life.

"Grace means that all of your mistakes
now serve a purpose instead of serving as
shame."
- Anne Lamott

Today's message
Your life is full of beauty. The problem happens
when you don't take notice of this beauty. Make
good choices and remember strength comes from
overcoming the things you once thought you could
not do. Don't give up. Hard work pays off in the end.
There are secret opportunities hidden inside every
failure. Everything comes to an eventual ending.
Make peace with the fact that you don't have to
worry, that everything will be ok for you. Sometimes
all you need to do is take a deep, cleansing breath.
Pick yourself up and trust that everything is
happening the way it is supposed to for you. Look
for the hidden beauty everywhere.

Ask yourself
How are my struggles and mistakes opportunities
for learning? I notice obstacles when I take my eyes
off my dreams; what are my dreams? How can I
challenge myself to be stronger and more graceful?

March 15

Release old anger, grief, and fear.

*"Every time you are tempted to react
in the same old way, ask if you want to be
a prisoner of the past
or a pioneer of the future."*
- Deepak Chopra

Remember

Negative emotions and grudges are a waste of the person you are. Honour and acknowledge negative emotions and learn the possible message and lesson from them but release long-held grievance stories that no longer serve you well. Sometimes you need to let go of things. You deserve the best things in your life; don't let anger and fear prevent you from experiencing good things. Distance yourself from people in your life who bother you and accept the positive, strong people you deserve. Ask yourself: What do I worry about? What blessings are surrounding me? Can I think of any hidden blessings in my life?

Affirm

I surround myself with good people.
I let go of negative toxic situations.
I release anger, fear, and grief.

March 16

Have the courage to
step out of the box.

*"Live your life the way you want.
You'll figure it out."*
- John Grisham

Today's message

You are in complete control of yourself. Growth in
your life has to start with your decision to move
forward beyond your current circumstances and
take ownership of your ability to do so. You don't
have to explain your dreams and aspirations to
anyone. You don't need approval from anyone to
live your life and do what makes you happy. It's time
to wake up and move the clouds out of the way of
your sunshine. Realize your potential and settle for
nothing less. Move out of your comfort zone. You
can only grow when you are willing to feel awkward
and uncomfortable while trying something new.

Ask yourself

How would I describe my character if I were cast in
a movie? What can I try that might be courageous?
How can I challenge myself today? How can I stand
up for my dreams and myself today?

March 17

Say affirmations regularly.

"Words have the power to both heal and destroy. When words are both true and kind, they can change our world."
- Unknown

Remember

Keep your eye out for positive events and occurrences during your day. Assume the best and see what happens. Think the best of yourself and others and look forward with hope to a great day. Affirm positive thoughts daily and keep focusing on what you do want. Affirmations are simply a declaration by a person that offers emotional support, focus, or encouragement. Tough times don't last. Look for things you can appreciate and be grateful for around you today to shift your energy. Affirm all the things you are thankful for and appreciate. What you focus on expands and directs your attention. Pay close attention to your repetitive thoughts. Make sure you keep thoughts on things your desire for yourself and your life.

Affirm

I believe good things happen.
I feel gratitude for waking up today.
Everything will be ok.
I affirm all that is positive and am grateful for the gifts in my life.

March 18

Pay attention to your thoughts.

"Whether you think you can
or think you can't, you're right."
- Henry Ford

Today's message

Trust your inner hunches and intuition. They are the best offers of guidance. Learn from within, and many ideas will come to you. All the answers you need ultimately come from inside you. Recognize when something is not good for you and be strong enough to let it go. You have trustworthy inspirations. Stop stopping yourself. Vision is the ability to see potential in what others overlook. A true tragedy in your life would be to let your talent die inside you. Awaken to your potential today. Only put blinders on those things that conspire to hold you back, especially the ones that are deep in your thinking. You have what you need within you.

Ask yourself

When you get confused, you can ask yourself: Whom am I listening to? What is my mind telling me? What song are my heart and mind singing? What is a good feeling thought?

March 19

Believe the best is yet to come.

"Nobody can go back and start a new beginning, but anyone can start today and make a new ending."
- Maria Robinson

Remember

Let negative experiences in your life motivate you to be better, stronger, and achieve more. Let go of feeling hurt or blaming others and focus on believing in yourself and all that you are. The more significant the obstacle, the greater the victory you will feel when you persevere and overcome the challenge. Don't be pushed by your problems or any obstacles. Be led by your dreams instead. Always remember the future will be fantastic if you can see possibilities before they are obvious. Look for possibilities and have faith in what will be. You are braver than you believe, stronger than you seem, and smarter than you think. You were given this life because you are strong enough to live it well. Don't be afraid to start over and have the chance to rebuild what you desire.

Affirm

I am a warrior.
I choose to focus on strength, courage, and power.
The worst is behind me, and great things are coming.

March 20

Use your power to
make your life better.

*"At any given moment you have
the power to say, this is not how
the story is going to end."*
- Christine Mason Miller

Today's message

Take responsibility for your thoughts, feelings and actions, and you will get your power back immediately. You are in charge of your life, and you cannot blame others for anything that is not working in your life. Your life is a result of your choices. If you are not happy with your life, make different choices. Connect with what you are passionate about. Everyday habits build the person you want to become. Think about you at your best, then think about all the necessary habits that will get you closer to that person you want to be. Use the power of daily routines to make your life better.

Ask yourself

Who am I when I am at my best? What decisions do I want to make today? Who do I want to be? What habits can I start today?

March 21

Discover what you love.

"Passion is the reason you journey.
Passion is the fire that lights your way."
- Zehner

Today's message
People with great passion can make the impossible happen. If you can't figure out your purpose, figure out your passion. Your passion will lead you right into your purpose. If life doesn't get better by chance, it will get better by change. Go back to your childhood wonder and make changes that bring about your passion. Approach life as if it is a continual stream of new beginnings. Make space in your life for new beautiful things to arrive. The joy of life comes from new opportunities and experiences. Keep growing and changing. Discover what you love and enjoy by trying new things and following what brings you joy or sparks your curiosity.

Ask yourself
What am I passionate about? When have I felt passionate? What brings me happiness and excitement? Who do I admire and wish I was more like? What can I take as inspiration for my own life?

March 22

Uplift, motivate, and comfort others.

"When life gives you a hundred reasons to cry, show life that you have a thousand reasons to smile!"
- Stephenie Meyer

Today's message
Being of service to others brings about a wonderful sense of compassion and empathy. You not only help others, but you feel a sense of connection and are uplifted. Thinking and being positive is not just about expecting good things to happen every time, but about accepting that whatever may occur is the best for that moment. You spread positivity by being supportive, kind, and optimistic. Every lousy situation and event will have something positive woven inside it at some point. Train your mind to see the good in every case and in every person. It will help others when going through struggles and have a profound impact. You never know who might need your support right now.

Ask yourself
How do I react to life? Who needs my support? There is a silver lining, or growth opportunity, in everything; am I willing to see it?

March 23

Do what makes you happy.

"The meaning of life is to find your gift.
The purpose of life is to give it away."
- Pablo Picasso

Remember

Do things that you love and do them with passion. You must have a strong desire to change and hope that it is greater than the desire to stay the same. The stronger your desire, the greater your motivation and achievement will be. Be open and willing to take whatever steps or inspirations call to you. Passion and purpose are simply about doing what you love and staying dedicated to following your dreams.

Affirm

I listen to my heart.
Today, I jump into my life with total effort.
I keep my desire in mind every day.
I am filled with gifts.
I choose to go with the flow of life.
My purpose and passion are revealing themselves to me.

March 24

Take notice of positive new experiences.

"Every day is a new beginning.
Take a deep breath and start again."
- Ritu Ghatourey

Today's message

Approach life as if it is a continual stream of new beginnings. Make space in your life for new beautiful things to arrive. Joy comes from new opportunities and experiences. Continue to grow and change. Let go of old things that don't serve you any longer. Embrace where you feel discontent. There is a saying that dissatisfied people end up changing the world. Being in a state of restlessness or discontent is a surprisingly good place since it is the first step towards change. When you have a strong ambition for things in your life, dissatisfaction is a symptom you might experience before taking action. Accept any feelings of discontent as a message that you need to fulfill your soul on a deeper level. Look for positive new experiences that feed you on that deep level.

Ask yourself

What feelings of frustration or dissatisfaction do I have? Can these help me by serving as growth? What do I want to come next for me? How can I stretch my mind today? What do I believe will come my way?

March 25

Release negative thoughts.

*"When you let go, you are creating
space for something better."*
- Unknown

Today's message

Everything in ife is a balance. There are things you can control and things you cannot. When you let go of the things you cannot control and manage your expectations, you will find peace. Replace any negative thoughts and things in your life with good thoughts and things that bring positive emotions like joy, happiness, and love. An excellent way to shift away from negative thoughts that might look like worry, an inner critic, or rumination, is to think of things that bring you joy. Shift to better feeling thoughts. Hear your negative thoughts and say, "I hear you. What are you trying to tell me?" Then decide to take action. What can you do? What feels better?

Ask yourself

How can I let life's events come in their own time and welcome all lessons? What am I trying to control in my life? What negative thoughts can I acknowledge and then shift towards better feeling thoughts?

March 26

Play and laugh.

*"Every laughing moment you have
leaves no room for stress."*
- Unknown

Today's message
Friendship is about showing up with love in times of
trouble. Keep those people in your life that make
you laugh, smile, and feel better. You deserve to be
happy and have some fantastic fun times in your life.
It's nice to have people in your life that would never
judge or criticize you. People will love you, not for
what you look like or accomplish, but for who you
are. Freshly see the world. Notice the humour in
things and choose to play, laugh, and have fun.
Make time for play, joy, and excitement. Adopt a
child-like playtime into your day. Break up your work
so you can laugh and have some stress-free time.
What makes you joyful? What are your quirks and
nerdy genius that makes you and others laugh? How
can you tap into that person today?

Ask yourself
What friend can I reach out to that will make me
smile and laugh? How can I be crazy, silly, and
carefree today? How do I make people laugh,
smile, and feel loved by being a friend?

March 27

See possibility.

"When you look at the possibilities instead of the problems, the future is filled with endless opportunities."
- Zig Ziglar

Remember

You have a wonderful life ahead of you. Look for possibilities and opportunities. Look for what inspires you and what you are passionate or excited about. Let joy be your magnet. Pay attention to all the possibilities, then follow what lights you up inside. It is up to you to believe great things can come to you. Looking for opportunity opens your mind and zooms out the lens to a place that is full of creativity. When you can broaden your mind, you see things that you may not have thought possible. Take time to be open to possibilities today. Today you can dream and envision those possibilities.

Ask yourself

What is possible? What are my dreams? What excites me? What are the options for me?

March 28

Don't let yourself feel isolated,
get out with others.

*"The best way to find yourself is to lose
yourself in the service of others."*
- Mahatma Gandhi

Today's message

When you open your heart and help others, you no longer feel alone. Connecting or helping others makes you happier and gives you endorphins that energize you. Serving others is good for your mental health and your well-being. You give your self-esteem and self-worth a boost when you serve others. Associate yourself with people of good qualities and form your community. Surrender yourself to people who make you feel touched and supported. Look for opportunities to get out and connect with other people. As humans, you are meant to be social and connected to other people. Seek kind and loving support from those around you. Someone out there cares for you, be sure to show that you care for others as well.

Ask yourself

Who can I choose to surround myself with? Am I the kind of person others want to be around?

March 29

Be vulnerable
and try new experiences.

*"This is about trying new things, getting
out of ruts and worry."*
- Teri Gault

Remember

Take time to respect other people's opinions and suggestions, even when you may disagree. They might have some insight that could help you in life. Allow yourself to be vulnerable as this is the place of learning, growth, and connection. The moment you take responsibility for everything in your life is the moment you can change anything in your life. You are in complete control of yourself. Growth in your life has to start with your decision to move forward beyond your current circumstances and take ownership of your ability to do so. Vulnerability is the birthplace of amazing things. You don't have to explain your dreams and aspirations to anyone. You don't need the approval of anyone to live your life and do what makes you happy. Be ok with being vulnerable and open to failing. It is the only way to learn and grow.

Affirm

I allow myself to be vulnerable.
I grow and learn every day.
I am open to trying new things.

March 30

Don't take yourself too seriously.

*"I laugh at myself. I don't take myself completely
seriously. I think that's another quality
that people have to hold on to ...
you have to laugh, especially at yourself."*
- Madonna

Today's message

Approach your day with a sense of humour and
lightness. Don't be hard on yourself or succumb to
drama. Surround yourself with funny people, watch
movies that make you laugh, and make light of tense
situations. Pay attention to and be a magnet to
funny things. Make your laugh happen a little harder
and a little longer! What you think of yourself is
much more important than what people think of
you. Don't be concerned with looking silly. Don't be
bothered by what other people may be thinking,
and don't take yourself too seriously. To not take
yourself too seriously, have some fun to look
forward to each day, and live in the present moment
as often as you can. Let go of grudges, and if you or
someone makes a mistake, decide to learn from it.

Affirm

I choose to laugh today.
I see the humour in life.
I approach myself with a light heart.
The most important opinion of myself is my own.

March 31

Take care of your body.

"Treat your body like the most amazing machine ever designed, because that's what it is."
- Nick Redmond

Today's message
The physical body is capable of so much, providing you with life. Be sure to nourish, respect, and appreciate it. With a healthy body, your mind and spirit can live with confidence. Expect more of yourself daily. Make good choices when it comes to eating, drinking, moving, and sleeping. Don't settle for less than you deserve because you deserve the very best that life has to offer. Self-love and self-control make your physical, mental, and emotional health a big priority in your life. Connect to nature and you will find beauty everywhere. Take time for rest when you need it. Get fresh air and take deep breaths.

Ask yourself
How can I keep my food, body, and thoughts clean? How can I make my environment feel calmer? What is my body needing right now? When can I make time to take a walk out in nature? What is the best way I can take care of my body today?

April 1

Withdraw your attention.

"Let her sleep, for when she wakes,
she will move mountains."
- Napoleon Bonaparte

Today's message
Rest time is not time wasted. It is an opportunity to gather strength and wisdom. Taking time to do nothing often brings everything back into perspective and helps you regain strength. Step back and evaluate what is essential. Taking time to self-reflect or examine is the key to insight and wisdom. You have probably heard the expression: *you can't pour from an empty cup.* Be sure to take care of yourself first. Discover all the things that make you feel full of life, love, and energy. Those are the things you want to do often. Conversely, notice the things that deplete or drain you, and when you need to step away and withdraw your energy from the world to go within. Try to avoid those things. Take time to turn inward and connect to what you are needing, wanting, and feeling.

Ask yourself
How can I listen to myself and take time to rest?
What are the best forms of rest for me?
Sometimes it is ok to take a step back; what do I need to do to withdraw?

April 2

Expect exciting opportunities.

"A year from now, everything you are stressing about won't even matter."
- Unknown

"The best wave of your life is still out there."
- Joel F. Crystal

Remember

Your thinking is like an architect for your life. Nobody can make you negative unless you decide to become negative. Your life is a direct result of the choices you make continuously. If you are not happy with your life, start to make better choices and look for opportunities. Like surfing, if you don't like the wave you just rode, get back out there and try another one. Exciting new opportunities are always around the corner. Observe ideas and thoughts that enter your mind. Pay attention to new beginnings, new ideas, and new energy, as they can be exciting. Ask yourself: What new ideas and choices can I entertain? What exciting opportunities might be coming my way?

Affirm

I monitor my thoughts.
I am positive and think about what I desire.
My mind is a powerful tool.

April 3

Stay optimistic and expect miracles.

*"Accept what is, let go of what was,
have faith in what will be."*
- Doris Day

Today's message

Don't give up on what is You; you will look back one day and be glad you didn't stop. At times you will face challenges and difficult situations. Like a caterpillar turns into a beautiful butterfly, your time to shine will come. Keep visualizing and embodying your success and take action daily towards your goals. Be sure to look for possibilities instead of perfection. There are opportunities everywhere, and if you don't see them, you have to create them for yourself. It is better to keep all your options open than to close your eyes and your thinking. Just remember, when nothing is entirely sure for you, anything is possible. Keep loving the life you have while creating the life you dream for yourself.

Ask yourself

Am I discouraged? What IS good now? How can I keep growing and preparing for my dreams? What would it take to visualize the things I want in my life: see it, feel it, and believe in it?

April 4

Follow your guidance.

"Trust your vibes. Energy doesn't lie."
- Unknown

Today's message

You know, deep down inside you, what to do at any given moment. Your inner voice and gut know best. Make sure you take time to slow down and listen to that inner voice. Often our inner voice is talking to us but other people's voices, opinions, and chatter can get in the way. Stay strong and connect to that voice that is YOURS. Everything in your life begins with an idea and a strong feeling. Dream big and act on your ideas. Don't let your fears hold you back from taking action towards your dreams. You can only achieve your dreams if you start believing in yourself. Follow your guidance and start to turn your ideas into actions. You know what to do. Ask yourself: What are my big dreams? What is my energy telling me?

Affirm

I listen to my voice.
I am wise.
I trust my vibes.
I know what to do.

April 5

Have a positive outlook.

"A happy person is not a person in a certain set of circumstances, but rather a person with a certain set of attitudes."
- Hugh Downs

Today's message

Objects and circumstances are not the things that make a person happy. It is our attitude and ability to see the world through a lens of appreciation and gratitude. Happiness comes from within and not from others. We have the choice to make ourselves happy or to make ourselves miserable. Don't wait for the right moment to start; shift your perspective to being grateful and look for good things in your life. This will evoke positive emotions such as joy, love, pleasure, and happiness.

Ask yourself

What makes me feel like sunshine? What do I appreciate about my life? What am I grateful for today? What can you do that will bring you joy?

April 6

Bring on your joy.

"Passion is energy. Feel the power that comes from focusing on what excites you."
- Oprah Winfrey

Remember

Never underestimate the power of all the things you have done. They are preparing you for a great future. Keep putting your attention and care into the things you want to grow in your life. What brings you joy? Follow your true passion and do the things in life you naturally enjoy. Your dream is going to bloom when it is ready. Enjoy the moment you are in now, and let joy be your magnet. What have you got to lose? Just go for it. Try that thing you have been nervous to try, talk to that person you've been avoiding, do something different today. There is so much joy to be had; you just need to follow that inkling. Today, bring on your joy.

Affirm

I am patient and growing every day.
I put attention on my dreams, I nurture my dreams.
I can do it.
I believe in myself today.
I try new exciting things.
I'm bringing on my joy.

April 7

Your prayers have been answered;
smile today.

*"Pray, not because you need something,
but because you have
so much to be thankful for."*
- Henri Nouwen

Today's message
Value and appreciate all the people, things, and experiences around you on a daily basis. Life goes by fast: take time to appreciate and love the moments. Give thanks for all the opportunities in your life. Even your struggles can lead to happiness. Choose to concentrate on the abundance in your life. Use your smile to change the world. Peace begins with a smile. Be happy with what you have in your life and catch yourself smiling.

Ask yourself
What are all the things I appreciate? What is going well for me? What do I love in my life? Where have my prayers been answered already? What makes me smile? How can I smile more often? What moments do I savour?

April 8

Have faith in yourself
and your abilities.

"Many people think they want things,
but they don't really have the strength,
the discipline. They are scared.
I believe that you get what you want
if you want it badly enough."
- Sophia Loren

Today's message

You are able to achieve anything you want. You have to be willing to invest the necessary energy, time, and effort in order to be successful. Follow your dreams and have faith in your abilities to accomplish great things. When you move into self-doubt, tap back into having faith in your abilities. Look for evidence of your success! Keep going. You have probably heard the saying: *I can. I will. End of the story.* You are capable of so much. Look your fear straight in the eye and notice how it might be trying to protect you or keep you safe, then ask it to back off a little so that you can move forward. Failure really isn't an option, as all failure is an opportunity to learn.

Ask yourself

Am I trying my hardest? What else can I do? How can I strengthen my abilities? What if failure was not an option?

April 9

Heal, bounce back,
and maintain inner peace.

"You cannot find peace by avoiding life."
- Virginia Woolf

*"The greatest glory in living lies not in
falling, but in rising every time we fall."*
- Nelson Mandela

Today's message

Try not to be in a hurry. Do everything quietly and in a calm spirit. Even when the world seems upsetting, try not to lose your inner peace. Even if your whole world seems upset, remember somewhere inside you there is a strength that will get you through everything. We cannot change the challenges and life experiences we have gone through, but we can learn and focus forward on the next exciting opportunity. Healing doesn't mean that damage and hurt never existed; it simply means that the challenge is no longer going to take control of your life.

Ask yourself

Do I have any wounds that need healing? How can I heal at my own pace? Life needs me; how can I heal, grow, and focus forward?

April 10

Trust everything falls into place and stand tall and confident.

"Be yourself.
Everyone else is already taken."
- Oscar Wilde

Today's message

There is a sense of peace in knowing that everything seems to fall into place. You've probably heard the expression: *storms don't last forever*. Just like every time you have been faced with a challenge, you got through it in the end; you can trust everything will work out for you. Take time to relax, even amid stress and challenge. You are safe and will be safe. Be humble in your confidence, yet courageous in your character. You just have to be yourself and go forward with confidence. Believe that you are enough and trust in your capabilities. Ask yourself: How can I tap into the things that make me special? When have I felt confident and proud?

Affirm

I am safe.
The challenge will pass.
I trust everything will be ok.
I am worthy.
I stand tall.

April 11

You are enough.

"If you correct your mind,
the rest of your life will fall into place."
- Lao Tzu

Today's message

You have enough strength inside you to face any adversity. You are enough. It doesn't have to make sense right now. Life is full of ups and downs. Let your brain relax. You don't need to stress. Find a place of peace within. Don't let the behaviour of others destroy your inner peace. Listen to your heart and quiet your mind. Look inside for happiness. Happiness is an inside job. No person, amount of money, or possession will make you happy. It is your own thinking that determines your own happiness. There are things you can do to make yourself happier, like practicing kindness, expressing gratitude, doing what you love and enjoy, and surrounding yourself with a great community of friends and family.

Affirm

I am enough.
I listen to my heart. I quiet my mind.
I am the only person that can make me happy.
I am in charge of my own life.
If I want a change, I can make it.

April 12

Remember lack only exists in the mind; think abundance.

"Worry never robs tomorrow of its sorrow; it only saps today of its joy."
- Leo Buscaglia

Remember
If you expect the best, you will be the best. Learn to use the power of your mind and positive thinking to change your life for the better. Focusing on lack or deprivation creates a pattern of lack and negative predictability. Instead, occupy your mind with abundance and anticipate good things. Never let the things you want make you forget about the things you already have. Take notice of all the good things in your life. Appreciate all the good things in your life. Having an attitude of gratitude becomes a daily practice. You can unwrap each day like a precious gift you have received - express gratitude for all things in your life. Deliberately notice the abundance in your life, and that is what you will see.

Affirm
I expect good things to come.
I notice the positives in my life.
I focus on abundance.

April 13

Challenge makes you stronger.

"If Positive Psychology teaches us anything, it is that all of us are a mixture of strengths and weaknesses. No one has it all, and no one lacks it all."
- Christopher Peterson

Today's message

Stress and challenges are inevitable in life, but suffering is an option. See your challenges as opportunities to be strong, learn, and grow. No matter how much it hurts now, someday you will look back and realize your struggles changed your life. Every struggle in your life has shaped you into the person that you are today. Although it is hard at times, you can be thankful for those challenges as they make you the person you are today and will be in the future. Look at all options. Until you believe you have options, you'll continue to feel stuck. When feeling confused or uncertain, try to look at all possible options. Zoom out the lens and try to see things from a different perspective. Consider what all your options are and what the possibilities might be in this situation.

Ask yourself

What more can I explore? What part of the situation have I not yet examined? What other angles can I think of?

April 14

Turn possibilities into realities.

"Nothing is impossible, the word itself says 'I'm possible!'"
- Audrey Hepburn

Remember

Look for possibilities, avoid searching for perfection. Keep an open mind when looking for opportunities. If you don't see any, get creative and make some for yourself. Don't close the door on new opportunities, you never know where they might lead you. Keep your options open and remember that anything is possible. There is an expression: *sometimes happiness is a feeling, and sometimes it is a decision*. You are in charge of your life. You get to decide what happens to a large degree. Make new realities for yourself. You are responsible for the actions you take. Take back your power and own the life that you are creating. Make some great choices today and every day!

Affirm

I see unlimited possibilities.
I have options to choose from.
I make changes in my life.
I am in charge of how I feel.
Today I am choosing happiness.
I make my own reality.

April 15

Enjoy the simple things.

"Delight in the little things."
- Rudyard Kipling

Today's message

Take delight in the simplest things in your life. Find the things and people that bring you great enjoyment and pleasure. No matter how serious life gets, you still need that time to be completely silly. The best times in life are the ones that are random and unplanned. Enjoy the simple things in your life that bring you joy!

Ask yourself

How can I be spontaneous? What would my inner child say to my adult self? Can I take a moment every day to deliberately notice at least one beautiful thing in my life? What am I grateful for in my life today? How can I choose to have a positive mind and a grateful attitude about my life? Where can I put my attention that makes me happy?

April 16

Enjoy music.

"Music is a piece of art that goes in the ears and straight to the heart."
- Blackmore

Today's message

Music can be a powerful tool to shift your emotions and feelings. Boost your mood with the power of music. Learn to let go of things and lift your emotions by listening to music. Mindfulness is paying attention to purpose in the present moment. Music is a wonderful tool that completely absorbs us and removes us from worry. Play with music and emotions. Listen to your favourite playlist. Make a playlist of music you love. What music moves you? Dance, sing, and play with music today.

Ask yourself

What music brings mindfulness and focus at the moment? What is my favourite music? Can I observe how music makes me feel and how it brings mindfulness? What music would I love to dance to?

April 17

Step outside.

"Those who don't believe in magic will never find it."
- Roald Dahl

Today's message

Playtime is a form of research, and it's amazing what you can discover. Fill your life with playfulness, and you will rediscover the magical world around you. Joy eases your life burdens and renews your sense of optimism as it makes you more open to new exciting possibilities. Sometimes a change of perspective is all it takes to see things in a positive light. Be open to life and step outside. Breathe in the fresh air. Look at the sky. Feel the sun on your skin. Take time to be outside and say yes to the beauty that nature can bring to you.

Ask yourself

What can I do to add more play, laughter, and joy into my life? Can I take a deep breath? Where can I go for a walk today? What can I say yes to today? When can I step outside?

April 18

Shine your bright light.

"Don't let someone dim your light simply because it's shining in their eyes."
- Jessica Ainscough

Today's message

Don't be afraid to be who you are and shine your bright light. You make the world a brighter place just by being you. Think about when you have been full of life and sparkle. What makes you shine bright? You have within you, right now, everything you need. Dare to live the life that you have dreamed of for yourself. Live out loud and do not dim down who you are meant to be for the sake of acceptance. Hold who you are in high regard. Ask yourself: I am strong and hold myself in high regard; how can I shine brightly today?

Affirm

I am enough.
I am full of sparkle and light.
Today, I shine my bright light.
I have all that I need within me

April 19

Dream.

*"Let your dreams be bigger
than your fears, and your actions
be louder than your words."*
- Unknown

Remember

Miracles happen when you expect them. Dare to live the life that you have dreamed of for yourself. Daily action towards your desires can make your dreams come true. The more clear you are about what you want in your life, the more likely you are going to achieve it. You are the creator of your life and your reality. What do you want your life to consist of? Your imagination is a wonderful tool for you to explore your options. Simply close your eyes and let your passion and imagination go wild today.

Ask yourself

What are my dreams? What do I want most for myself? What have I done today to make my dreams come true? What is possible? What do I see when I close my eyes? What is exciting about the future?

April 20

Go with the flow and be open to life.

"Life is a journey with problems to solve, lessons to learn, but most of all, experiences to enjoy."
- Ritu Ghatourey

Today's message

Wanderlust isn't about running away from everything. It is about taking time to experience the outside world, to discover and experience *you*. Look forward to new opportunities, and when they come along, you have to grab them. If opportunities don't come along, go find them. As you say yes to life, the more life will say yes to you. You will enjoy life a lot more by saying yes instead of saying no. Saying yes to happiness means learning to say no to the things and people that stress you out or bring you down. Opportunity does not necessarily knock at your door; it presents itself when you open it.

Ask yourself

What fears do I have? What fears might be holding me back from opportunities and adventure? What would I do if I were not scared? What can I say "yes" to? What new experience can I try? What action can I take to dissolve my fears?

April 21

So much in store for you.

*"When someone you have a lot of respect for believes in you,
it helps you believe in yourself."*
- Cat Osterman

Remember
Sometimes we doubt our capabilities and question our strength. Reach out to those that believe in you, that inspire you, and that you are inspired by. Ultimately, it is up to you to believe great things are in store for you. Listen to the support and encouragement from others! It is up to you to believe great things can come to you. Today, ask some of the most special people in your life what they value about you, have them write it down. Then, reflect on their powerful message. Sometimes others believe in you more than you believe in yourself. There is so much in store for you!

Ask yourself
What possible opportunities do I see? What is my dream? What is exciting to me about this?

Affirm
Things are about to get really good.
I am so excited for all the good things to come to me.
I keep my chin up.

April 22

Rest for now.

*"I just need a break from everything
for a little while."*
- Unknown

Remember

Sometimes the easiest and best way to solve a problem is to stop, step away, and stop participating in the problem. Know when to step away from the busyness of life and gain perspective. Withdraw your attention from the world around you and never neglect an opportunity for improvement. It is ok to close your eyes and take a break. Your life can easily become busy and chaotic; stepping back for some rest and replenishing is essential. Take the time you need to replenish and regain some clarity and perspective. Take a few deep breaths, meditate, take a nap, or simply lie down. Take some time to rest your body and your mind today.

Affirm

I need rest.
Today, I give myself permission to have moments where I do nothing.
I step back today and self-examine.
I listen to my body and mind.
I build my resources with rest.

April 23

Notice repetition.

"Synchronicity is the universe saying you are getting warmer."
- Michelle Risi

Today's message

Pay attention to meaningful coincidences in your life. Notice meaningful connections and messages that happen all around you. Serendipity is the fortunate discovery, seemingly by chance, of something or someone that leads to other wonderful things happening in your life. Pay attention to repetition or coincidences! Trust in the messages around you. Seeing things more than once can spark an interest and encourage research for potential underlying messages. Have fun with serendipity.

Ask yourself

Can I see any patterns and messages? What am I ready for? Can I think of times of coincidences? How can I notice the wonder and miracles in my life? What neat things have happened around me lately?

April 24

Fill yourself up today.

"You can't pour from an empty cup.
Take care of yourself first."
- Expression

Today's message

Discover all the things that make you feel full of life, love, and energy. These are the things you want to do often. Conversely, notice the things that deplete or drain you, and try to avoid these things. Balance is not something that you find; it is something that you have to create. If your life feels like something is missing, seek balance. Make sure you have a nice blend of fun, friends, family, nature, exercise, and rest. Build habits in your day that restore your energy and vitality. Today, think about and do the things that bring balance and fill you up.

Affirm

I choose to do things that fill me up today.
I do less of the things that drain me and more of the things that energize me.
I take care of myself.
I choose balance in my life.
I give areas of my life attention that need it.
My life is balanced with work and play.

April 25

Everything has perfect timing.

"Creativity is intelligence having fun."
- Albert Einstein

Today's message

Creative thinking inspires new ideas, and ideas inspire change. An essential part of being creative is not being afraid to fail. Rearrange what you know. Find out what you may not have thought of already: this is creativity. When you are stressed, you block the flow of creativity. Think about all the things that are going well for you right now and notice all the love that surrounds you. It is up to you to believe things are on their way and happening for you on their own time. Take the moments that you are in and make them meaningful. Trust that patience and faith will pay off for you. Imagination is the beginning of creation. Creativity is like the incentive for improvement. Have fun exploring opportunities. Remember, worrying will not stop negative things from happening, but it will stop you from enjoying the good things in your life.

Ask yourself

What can I do to be creative today? Can I think of some creative opportunities for my life? What options can I create?

April 26

Leave everyone better than you found them.

"We rise by lifting others."
- Robert Ingersoll

Today's message
Use your smile to change the world. Peace begins with a smile. Be happy with what you have in your life and catch yourself smiling. Positivity is contagious, and so is negativity. Choose to spend more time with people who think positively, speak positively, and support you. And be the same for others.

Ask yourself
What makes me smile? How can I smile more often? What moments do I savour?

Remember
When you are a person that lifts others up, you spread happiness and kindness throughout the world and create a ripple effect. Remember to nurture and build people up. Be one who has an understanding heart and looks for the best in people.

April 27

Choose peace.

"Worrying doesn't take away tomorrow's troubles; it takes away today's peace."
- Unknown

Today's message

It is possible to choose peace over worry. Today try not to stress over things you cannot control. If you are searching for the one person that will change your life, take a look in the mirror. There are things you can do to make yourself happier, like practicing kindness, expressing gratitude, doing what you love and enjoy, and surrounding yourself with a great community of friends and family. Take time to look around you for great things. Appreciate the miracle that life brings. You can find evidence to prove anything. Look for evidence of peace and beauty in your life. The more you look, the more your find!

Remember

You can choose to be calm, patient, faithful, and hopeful in moments of stress. Shift your focus to gratitude and curiosity for instant peace.

Affirm

I am in charge of my life.
I am in charge of my own happiness.
I choose to be peaceful.
If I want to change, I can.

April 28

Focus on effort and determination.

*"If you work hard enough
and assert yourself, you can shape
the world to your desires."*
- Malcolm Gladwell

Today's message

Talent is a funny thing. The harder people practice and work, the more their talent seems to stand out. Hard work, passion, and practice pay off. Every expert was at one time a beginner. You are capable of anything. Focus on the process instead of the end result. Keep practicing and getting better. Put effort into what matters the most for you. Practice and effort combined with your passion and talent will get you very far. Today, look at the things you want to learn, grow, and nurture with your focus and effort. Check-in with yourself and your life, and determine how you need to show up today? How you show up will have an impact on your day. Trust your gut instinct and figure out what would best serve you today. What do you want to focus your efforts towards? Who do you want to be today?

Affirm

I choose to focus on effort.
Effort and practice bring me skills.
I can do anything if I learn and practice.
Talent without practice is wasted.

April 29

Enjoy your life.

"There are two things in life that motivate you: the fear of pain and the desire for pleasure."
- Anthony Robbins

Today's message

Take the time to enjoy the simple things and find happiness in the common things in your life. At this moment where you are, try to be fully present. Take time to relax. Try not to take life so seriously that you start to forget the whole point is to enjoy it and have fun. Try new things today. If you don't try new novel things, your life can get boring. You never know if you will enjoy something until you try it. Life brings you new experiences and opportunities. Be sure to seize every chance you get to try something new. You will learn and grow as a result. Life brings good experiences, so be open to new adventures and wonderful changes.

Ask yourself

What's my guilty pleasure? How can I remind myself that life is supposed to be fun? How can I have fun, be crazy, and be silly today? What can you try today? What fun new things can you plan?

April 30

Balance.

*"A mind open to alternative perceptions is
a mind aligned with love."*
- Unknown

Today's message
Keep your mind open to many opportunities. Be
prepared to look at many options and from different
perspectives. When you open your mind, your world
will open up to you. Sometimes we feel stuck
because our thinking is stuck. Balance your life by
looking at new perspectives. A sense of peace
comes when you can see many possibilities. Today,
seek to understand and walk through your day in a
curious way.

Ask yourself
What else can I consider? How would it look if I
looked at this differently? What am I missing here?

Affirm
I choose balance in my life.
I give areas of my life attention that need it.
My life is balanced with work and play.
I balance talking with listening.

May 1

Stand tall and take initiative.

*"Don't wait for the perfect moment.
Take a moment and make it perfect."*
- Zoey Sayward

Today's message
Take responsibility and initiative for yourself today.
Don't blame anyone else for your circumstances.
Your successes and accomplishments are your
responsibility. Take the initiative of believing in
yourself and take responsibility for your own life. Do
the work your need to do and persist. Ask yourself:
When have I felt confident and proud? What action
will I take today? What can I take the initiative on in
my life?

Remember
Be humble in your confidence yet courageous in
your character. You just have to be yourself and go
forward with full confidence. Believe that you are
enough and trust in your capabilities. Take
responsibility for your reality and initiative for
making positive changes.

Affirm
I am worthy.
I stand tall.
I am sweet and caring to others.

May 2

Notice your progress.

"Good things happen when you set your priorities straight."
- Scott Cann

Today's message

You are stronger than you think. Look at all the things you have already accomplished and gotten through successfully. You are great, never doubt yourself. Give yourself credit and acknowledgment for how far you have progressed. You are a work in progress. Notice where you are currently and be sure to give yourself grace along your path.

Ask yourself

What am I most proud of? What challenges have I overcome in the past? What allows me to believe in myself?

Remember

Whenever you find yourself doubting how far you can go, just remember how far you have already come. Look to the past for evidence as to just how far you have come. Remember everything you have faced, all the challenges and battles you have won, and all the fears you have overcome. Take a life review and notice your progress.

May 3

You matter.

"It doesn't matter what others are doing.
It matters what YOU are doing."
- Unknown

Today's Message

Don't worry about what others think. Also, try not
to compare yourself to what others are doing. You
will feel more at peace if you just focus on yourself
and stay positive. Keep moving forward, and don't
concern yourself with what anybody thinks. Do what
you have to do for you. Don't let other people
destroy your inner peace and confidence. Be
courageous and do what you're afraid to do. Refrain
from comparing yourself to others and focus on
yourself. Don't be scared to give up things in your
life to go for what could be fantastic. The most
powerful relationship that you will have is the one
that you have with yourself. When you know you
matter, the love and attention that you can give
yourself are priceless. What can you do today to
show yourself that you matter?

Affirm

I do me.
I choose to focus on myself.
I am doing great things.
I compare for inspiration.

May 4

State your desires and make a wish.

"A dream is a wish your heart makes."
- Mack David (Cinderella)

Today's message

You are given a wish because you have the power to make it come true. Everything you can imagine is confirmed; your wishes can come true. Don't complain that wishes don't come true if you are unwilling to take action towards your dreams. When you get clear on what you desire, be sure to embody or feel this dream as if it were already real. Having those feelings will make you see evidence that your vision is possible. Then take your dream visioning one step further and try to see the process it takes to reach this dream. Notice the process involved and the action that you can take today to make that dream come true. You have probably heard the expression: *dreams only work if you do*.

Remember

Life has no limitations except the ones you make yourself. Know your limits but never stop trying to exceed and push yourself through them. Live your dreams, make your wishes, and take risks. Imagination can take you to worlds you have not yet thought were possible and make them real.

May 5

Be nice to yourself.

*"If you wouldn't say it to a friend,
don't say it to yourself."*
- Jane Travis

Today's Message
The way that you speak to yourself about yourself matters. Your words have an impact on your strength, confidence, and level of happiness. When you are mad or disappointed in yourself or a situation, think about the words you are about to choose before you speak. Talk to yourself like you would talk to someone that you love. Your mental health is very important, and negative, mean words can affect you adversely. Repetitive self-talk is a powerful form of communication because it can empower you or tear you down. Practice some self-compassion where you are kind towards yourself when you are suffering or upset. You acknowledge your common humanity and are mindful of the situation and inner dialogue.

Affirm
I speak kind words to myself.
I filter my mental chatter.
I am kind to myself.
I enjoy being nice to myself.

May 6

Look up and choose peace.

"A joyful life is an individual creation that cannot be copied from a recipe."
- Mihaly Csikszentmihalyi

Today's message
It is possible to choose peace over worry. Today try not to stress over things you cannot control. Decide to choose peace and be peaceful today! Lift your head when you're down. You have to fight through some bad days to earn the best days. There is a lot of beauty and peace in the sky. Choose to see the awe of the world around you. Look at the sky or out into nature and you will be transformed. Take a deep breath and look up. Enjoy your own life and your own personal recipe you have created.

Remember
You can choose calm, patience, faith, and hope in a moment of stress. Shift your focus to gratitude and the beauty around you for instant peace.

Affirm
I choose peace.
I am calm and faithful.
I keep looking up.
I follow my own recipe.

May 7

Be positive and feel positivity.

"We're so busy watching out for what's just ahead of us that we don't take time to enjoy where we are."
- Calvin & Hobbes

Remember

Take time to look around you for great things. Appreciate the miracle that life brings. You can find evidence to prove anything. Look for evidence of positivity in your life. The more you look, the more you will find! Your mind is a powerful thing. When you fill it with positive thoughts and direct your thoughts onto good things, your life will start to change. Your attitude and what you focus on determine your direction and how you feel. Think positive and talk positive and feel positive. Train your mind to see and look for the positive in every situation. You are the master of your mind. Don't think about what might go wrong, but rather think about what might go right for you. Try to balance out our natural negativity bias by striving to seek out positive emotional thoughts.

Affirm

I am excited about new possibilities.
I take notice of all the good things that come to me.
I see positive things all around me.
I choose to focus on the positive.

May 8

Be strong and disciplined.

"Being strong doesn't mean you don't feel pain. It means you feel it and try to understand it so that you can grow from it."
- Karen Salmansohn

Today's Message

The best way to approach obstacles in your life is to use them as an opportunity to learn. See challenge as an opportunity to learn and grow. Stay firm in your belief in yourself while seeing the challenge from a growth mindset. See every mistake from the perspective of making progress and getting better. This approach to the challenge will bring you a sense of peace and strength. Motivation sometimes might die off, but discipline and habit can take their place. Maintain your power and intention to start living the life you always imagined. Don't let obstacles or setbacks hold you back. You don't have to be perfect, and you will make mistakes; be brave enough to start and keep going. You are strong and disciplined.

Affirm

I am strong and disciplined.
I am learning and growing, life is my classroom.
I make today ridiculously amazing.
I am impeccable and take action.

May 9

Relax and love yourself.

"You have enough. You do enough.
You are enough. Relax."
- Unknown

Remember

Find some time to relax, play, and laugh. While seeking and accomplishing your dreams, don't forget to enjoy life. Don't be too hard on yourself today. Notice where you have been pushing hard. You don't have to wait for or make everything perfect before you decide to enjoy life a little. Take time to sit back and relax. Recharge your strength with downtime. Work on being in love with the person in the mirror. Don't limit yourself because of what people might think or your own high expectations. Sometimes it is essential to relax and love yourself simply. Relaxing is an integral part of seeking out your dreams. Take time to catch your breath today.

Affirm

It's time to have some fun.
Today, I enjoy the little things in my life.
I am listening to my need to relax.
It's okay to close your eyes.
I am worthy of loving myself.
I see love all around me.

May 10

Lighten up.

*"Life is too important
to be taken seriously."*
- Oscar Wilde

Today's message

To attract positive energy and positive things into your life, you need to give off positive energy. You have the choice to make things easy, to lighten up. Try not to take things personally or take life too seriously. If you are caught in the grips of taking life too seriously, soften your heart and mind. Never get jealous when you see someone having fun; just create your own fantastic fun time. Sometimes you might just need to have some fun and shift your focus. Life can get very disciplined and full of to-do lists; take time to step away and see the lighter side of it all. Try to be silly and soft with yourself and others today. It will freshen up your life.

Ask yourself

What can I choose to let go of? What makes me smile and enjoy myself? If you stopped having fun, ask yourself: What would be fun for me to do today?

May 11

Choose a good life and be curious.

"We are not given a good life or a bad life. We are given a life, and it's up to us to make it good or bad."
- Gautama Buddha

Today's Message

Happiness is a choice and not a result of getting something or achieving something. Nothing will make you happy and content until you choose to be happy and satisfied. You can change what you focus on and choose to be in a happier, more content state. With our peace of mind and thoughts, we have the control to find inner peace and happiness. You can experience inner peace the second you decide you control your thinking and focus. Success comes from taking risks knowing that they might fail. Take the steps you need to take, and imagine all that is possible. Your future and a good life are created by all the little things you do today. Lead yourself to new opportunities. Remain curious, and all kinds of interesting new things will present themselves to you.

Affirm

I choose to see happiness and my good life.
My life is beautiful.
I am curious and ready to try new things.

May 12

Try new things
and fix what is broken.

*"If you never try, you'll never know what
you are capable of."*
- John Barrow

Today's message

Life brings you new experiences and opportunities. Be sure to seize every chance you get to try something new. You will learn and grow as a result. Make peace with your broken pieces. Life brings good experiences, so be open to new adventures and beautiful changes. Life will also get challenging at times. Remember that sometimes good things fall apart to make room for something better. Remain open to new things.

Affirm

I choose to try new things.
I see my life as an opportunity to try.
I learn and grow every day.

Ask yourself

What needs my attention? When I feel I'm falling apart, what helps me get back together? What new opportunity can I try?

May 13

Appreciate your life and celebrate.

"The more you praise and celebrate your life, the more there is in life to celebrate."
- Oprah Winfrey

Today's message

When you are grateful for all the things in your life, you will find that fear fades and abundance appears. Be happy and express gratitude. It will open the door to abundance in your life. Your abundant attitude is like a magnet that will draw positive things and people to you. In psychology, it is called a confirmation bias. You notice the things in your world that confirm your thinking. Life isn't always perfect, but it's always what you make of it. Good times, fun friends, and family make the best memories. When life is sweet, be thankful and celebrate. When life is harsh, be grateful and learn. You can unwrap each day like a precious gift that you have received - express gratitude for everything in your life.

Ask yourself

Can I take a moment every day to deliberately notice at least one beautiful thing in my life? What am I grateful for in my life today? How can I choose to have a positive mind and a grateful attitude about my life?

May 14

Take ownership of your life and
create your happiness.

*"Until you take ownership for your life, you
will always be chasing happiness."*
- Sean Stephenson

Remember

You are in the driver's seat of your life. You decide
what happens to a large degree. You are responsible
for the actions you take. Take back your power and
own the life that you are creating. You can't change
your genes or specific circumstance, but you do
have control over intentional behaviours, and they
can have a significant impact on your life. Our
thoughts, actions, and growth impact our life. Make
some great choices today and every day! Taking
your life into your own hands is taking responsibility
for the good and bad you live. You can create more
happiness by taking the initiative and ownership of
your reality.

Affirm

I am in charge of how I feel.
Today, I am choosing my happiness by taking back
ownership of my reality.
I make my reality.

May 15

Spread your wings and fly.

"Until you spread your wings, you'll have no idea how far you can fly."
- Bonaparte

Today's message

Every day you have a choice: you can look for obstacles or opportunities. Life feels much nicer when you are continuously asking yourself, what are the options here? Don't let fear of what may happen to get in the way or hold you back from following your heart and dreams. Every new experience is an opportunity to learn and grow. It's okay to be scared or nervous; it means that you are about to do something brave and courageous. Believe in great things for yourself. What would it look like to spread your wings and fly?

Ask yourself

Are my insecurities holding me back? Is anyone or anything holding me back from my dreams? What opportunities can I create? What are the opportunities in my life? What are the challenges I can learn from? What great things can I look forward to?

May 16

Don't compare and stay confident.

"Note to self: Don't measure your progress using someone else's ruler."
- Unknown

Today's Message

It never feels good to compare yourself to others. Comparison can make you struggle and feel insecure. When we compare ourselves to others, we tend to measure ourselves up against that person. By not comparing, you are choosing peace and allow yourself to focus on your own story. This self-focus will enable you to peacefully be the unique you that only you can be! Self-confidence is the best outfit, rock it and own it. Try to stay in your lane and put blinders on if you need to limit distractions. It is who you think you are not that is upsetting when you compare. Do what you can to restrict social comparison and focus on yourself. If you do compare, frame it in such a way that you are looking for inspiration. Compare only to get inspired, be happy for others and say to yourself, "more of that for me too, please."

Affirm

I am unique and original.
I am on my path and progressing at my own pace.
I stay in my lane and only compare for inspiration.

May 17

Think happy, be happy.

"Once you start making the effort to 'wake yourself up' - that is, be more mindful in your activities - you suddenly start appreciating life a lot more."
- Robert Biswas-Diener

Today's message
Beautiful things happen when you distance yourself from negativity and be somebody who makes everybody feel good. Happiness is a choice, and it starts with what you focus your attention on and what you are thinking. Take notice of what's good in your life, be grateful, and practice being happy. Think happy thoughts, and you will feel positive emotions. When you think you're not satisfied with your life, know that your happiness depends on your thinking. What might be a better feeling thought? Monitor your emotions today and notice what thought made you feel this way. Shift your thinking to better feeling thoughts.

Ask yourself
How does that thought make me feel? What is incredible in my life? Where can I put my attention that makes me happy? What brings me more happiness?

May 18

Be open to life and imagine what is possible.

"If you believe in yourself, anything is possible."
- Miley Cyrus

Today's message

You will enjoy life a lot more by saying yes and imagining what is possible for you. Saying yes to what is possible for you means you are learning to try, learn, and grow. Opportunity does not necessarily knock at your door; it presents itself when you open it. Don't be afraid to try something new; when you do, you can only grow. Keep imagining what is possible for you. Do the things you love without any doubt. Don't be afraid to change; it will lead you to new beginnings and opportunities. Be curious, try new things, ask questions, and be open to what life may bring you.

Ask yourself

What can I say yes to? What new experience can I try? What action can I take to dissolve my fears?

Affirm

I take a risk and enjoy the rewards.
I remain curious and intrigued in my life.
I imagine great possibilities for myself.

May 19

Test the limits and breakthrough.

"Learn something new.
Try something different.
Convince yourself that you have no limits."
- Brian Tracy

Ask yourself
How can I push myself beyond my perceived limits?
What limits have I created in my mind? How can I
break free and step beyond limitations?

Remember
Live your life and break free from your rut and
change your life forever. When you add some
novelty or something new into your life, you will
achieve a sense of accomplishment. This feeling of
achievement makes you feel alive. Refuse to be
average. Let your heart and spirit soar as high as you
can. Always just be yourself, express yourself, and
have faith in yourself. Sometimes you might hold
back and stay where things seem comfortable.
When you test your perceived limits, amazing things
happen to your confidence and ability to believe in
yourself.

Affirm
Today, I express myself fully.
I am ready to spread my wings and fly.
I have no limits, and I am extraordinary.

May 20

Focus on what's important.

"Life is like a camera...
Focus on what's important.
Capture the good times.
Develop from the negatives.
And if things don't work out,
take another shot."
- Unknown

Today's message

Sometimes you will want to take a step back and realize what is essential in your life: what you want to live with and what you can't live without. Don't complicate your life; decide what's important and build your life around that. You get to choose where you focus your attention and what is important to you. What you decide to focus on is what you will see. There is a confirmation bias in psychology, where you will look for and see things to confirm your thinking. Be very careful what you put your focus on in your day. Try to stay focused on the crucial matters at hand.

Ask yourself

What is important? What do I have the courage to create for myself? What do I need to let go of? Where does my attention go? If my attention goes in a direction I prefer not to go, what will I do to change the channel and focus?

May 21

Be careful of your thoughts.

"Sometimes it's the smallest decisions that can change your life forever."
- Keri Russell

Today's message

When feeling confused or uncertain, you can try to look at all possible options. Zoom out the lens and try to see things from a different perspective. Your life may not be flawed, but your thinking might be. It is incredible how repetitive thoughts become beliefs and beliefs become emotions and actions. Tend to what you keep repeating that may be holding you back. Change your thinking, and you can change the way you see yourself and the world. If you think positive thoughts and possibilities, your life and perception of yourself will be positive and open to possibilities. Monitor your thoughts. Thoughts become emotions, and emotions drive action.

Ask yourself

What could I explore? What part of the situation have I not yet considered? What is another way to look at this? What is the story I am telling myself about myself? What do I hold on to, that I need to let go of? What are some better feeling thoughts?

May 22

Challenge makes you stronger, but you can't be strong all the time.

"What doesn't kill you make you stronger, stand a little taller."
- Kelly Clarkson

Today's message
It's okay not to be okay. Stress and challenges are inevitable in life, but suffering is an option. See your challenges as opportunities to be strong. No matter how much it hurts now, someday you will look back and realize your struggles changed your life for the better. Being strong means sometimes admitting you are not okay. You may need help or support. Remind yourself that it is impossible to be happy all the time. Break down, cry yourself to sleep, be upset. We all are human beings, not robots. It is perfectly okay to feel broken at times.

Remember
Although it can be hard, you can be thankful for those challenges as they make you stronger every day. It is equally important to give yourself permission to be human and honour your feelings.

Affirm
I am okay with not being okay.
My emotions are communicating.
I trust my feelings.

May 23

Be spontaneous and
put your life in motion.

*"The biggest adventure you can take is to
live the life of your dreams."*
- Oprah Winfrey

Remember

There is an expression: *overplanning kills the magic*.
Overplanning and perfection can be paralyzing. Take
time to remember what childhood delight brought
you happiness; chances are it will still bring you
excitement. Be spontaneous, sometimes later
becomes never. When you do things with no
explanation but just with spontaneity, you can be
sure that you enjoy yourself. Let certainty and
uncertainty feed off each other and find your child-
like wonder. Put your life into motion; your passion
makes you want to give your all. Now is the time to
make your next ten years unforgettable. Keep
moving forward in the direction of your dreams and
put everything unrelated aside. You do not need to
over-plan or hesitate. Today, put your life in motion.

Affirm

I take delight in my life.
Today, I sprinkle my life with a bit of silliness.
I am spontaneous, and there is no better time for
me.

May 24

Be happy for others.

"Admire other people's beauty and talent without questioning your own."
- Brooke Hampton

Today's message

Beauty is all around you so take the time to notice and enjoy the magnificence. Life is a series of thousands of tiny miracles. Notice and savour the miracles, big and small. Don't compare yourself with anyone else in this world. Only compare to the person you were yesterday. If you look to others, notice the beautiful, beautiful things for them and celebrate with them. Beauty is all around you. Take time to open your eyes, and you will notice and experience more beauty.

Ask yourself

What is beautiful in my life? If I were to be an outsider dropped into my life, what would they find beautiful and unique? What is beautiful in other's lives that I can celebrate as well? When good things happen to others, how can I be enthusiastic for them?

May 25

Permission to be human.

"It's great to be great,
but it's greater to be human."
- Will Rogers

Today's message

Maybe you don't have perfect hair, flawless skin, or perfect teeth; that doesn't mean you're not beautiful. Perhaps you didn't handle a situation as well as you wish you could have; that doesn't mean you're not a good person. Permit yourself to be human! Practice a sense of grace and softness with yourself. Give yourself the okay and compassion to make mistakes. You are human, and you will not be perfect all the time. You will make mistakes, fall, an d feel inadequate at times. Practice self-compassion and give yourself an understanding of what it is like to be human. Be kind towards yourself today and every day.

Remember

You come to love yourself and others not by finding the perfect person but by seeing yourself and others as perfectly imperfect. Vulnerability is the acknowledgment that you are human.

Affirm

I am not perfect, and that is okay, I am human.
I avoid judging and admit we are all human.

May 26

Pay close attention.

"You have to pay attention, get yourself ready for anything because you don't know what is going to happen."
- Mark Adams

Today's message

When you pay attention, it is incredible how much you end up learning. It's sweet when someone remembers every little detail about you, not because you keep reminding him or her, but because they pay attention. Listen to your heart and pay attention to your intuition. There is an expression: *you have two ears and one mouth for a reason.* It Implies the importance of listening more than you talk. You can gain a lot of perspective by being curious and listening to others. Pay close attention to details and be mindful of yourself as well. Try to be mindful and present in conversation today and notice how much more meaningful the connection feels.

Ask yourself

What is life teaching me right now? How can I be more mindful and present in my interactions? What would happen if I spoke less and listened more?

May 27

Do something scary.

*"Courage is being scared to death
but saddling up anyway."*
- John Wayne

Today's message

Try something new and slightly scary today. You will be amazed how facing your fears and pushing through them will bring you to new levels in your life. You will feel a sense of accomplishment and achievement. Trying something slightly scary will build your confidence in trying new things. Start small and grow your confidence by trying difficult things. Great things come out of testing your abilities.

Remember

Always do things that are within safety and that will move you forward towards your goals. Could you ask that guy or girl out? Book a flight somewhere? Send an email asking for that favour? What have you been putting off out of fear?

Ask yourself

What would scare me slightly that I could do today? What small thing would represent a victory? What have I been putting off that I can try?

May 28

Choose to make yourself strong.

"We either make ourselves miserable,
or we make ourselves strong.
The amount of work is the same."
- Carlos Castenada

Today's message

When things are not going as well as expected or desired, choose to take those moments to make yourself better and stronger. Decide to build into yourself the qualities and characteristics you need that will help you to be stronger. What will build you up today? Learning, growing, and taking opportunities to build your strength are elements of well-being.

Remember

Choose to build yourself up in times of challenge or struggle. In the long run, working on making yourself better will feel better. No one will be as invested in you as you can be for yourself. Choose today to invest in your success. Even tiny little things can build you up. What has helped you to feel strong in the past?

Ask yourself

What can I do to make myself stronger? What always makes me feel better? Is there something I can do to build myself up?

May 29

Make good choices.

"You have brains in your head. You have feet in your shoes. You can steer yourself any direction you choose."
- Dr. Seuss

Ask yourself
What is important to me? How can I follow my own heart, live my passion and find deep meaning? How do I know I'm making good choices?

Remember
We are all confronted with countless choices each day. The key is to honour your priorities and be brave enough to let go of what isn't working in your life. You deserve happiness, and deep down inside, you know what you need to do. What are some of the good choices you have made in the past that have led to good outcomes? What great choices can you make today that will lead you to the person you desire to be? You create your reality with the choices that you make today. These choices repeated become habits, and habits help you reach your goals over time.

Affirm
Today, I am a priority.
I choose to follow my heart, make good choices.
I let go of what isn't serving me.

May 30

Cheer up those around you.

"Try to be a rainbow in someone's cloud."
- Maya Angelou

Today's message
You can make a difference in someone's life by being beautiful, kind, lovely, supportive, and compassionate. Kindness is not only good for the person you are kind towards, but it is also good for your well-being. Being kind brings about positive emotions. When we fill our day with more positive emotions like joy, love, happiness, and care, we beautifully experience our world.

Remember
You may not know or understand what someone is dealing with in life, but you can make a huge impact. You might be the highlight that changes the trajectory of a persons' life. You never know the effects that you can have on someone's life. Find reasons to be kind to others today and every day.

Ask yourself
Is there someone that needs cheering up? How can I be kind and helpful to someone? How can I be more compassionate? How does being kind feel to me?

May 31

Connect to what brings you joy.

"Change is the essence of life;
be willing to surrender who you are
for what you could become."
- Norman Vincent Peale

Today's message
You become light by doing the things that spark the light inside you. The first step to getting where you want to go is having the courage to get rid of what you don't want. If you don't like something in your life, change it. You have probably heard the expression: *when one door closes, another one opens*. The great news is that doors will open for you. Sometimes you need to close doors to make room for new doors to open for you. The emotion of joy is an excellent indication tool to help you navigate where you want your life to head. Connect to the people, places, and things that bring you joy today and every day.

Ask yourself
What brings me joy? What can I do that brings me towards my goals? What do I want to become?

June 1

Endings and new beginnings.

"Be kind to yourself while you adjust."
- Unknown

Remember

There are times in your life when you need to walk away from things so that you can move forward to something even better. Never give up. There is a natural flow of beginnings and endings. Take notice of the cycles, and as one thing is ending, be excited about the new beginnings. It is a natural cycle in life. When you feel upset about something ending or what has taken its course, remember: the end of one thing is the start of something else new and exciting. Lovingly let go of what you need to let go of and make room for something new. What cycle is ending in your life, and what new beginning can you look forward to today? You might need extra compassion and inner nurturing during this cycle and time of change.

Affirm

I am excited about new beginnings.
I wipe my slate clean, I start fresh.
I lovingly accept the natural cycles in my life.
I am kind to myself through the process of change.

June 2

Fill your cup.

*"What if we recharged ourselves
as often as we did our phones?"*
- Unknown

Today's Message

There is an expression: *the best way to recharge
your batteries is to unplug from the world for a
while*. Make yourself a priority and take time to turn
inward. Do something just with yourself and be ok
with being alone with yourself. It will help to
recharge your batteries and give you a hefty dose of
self-care. Take a yoga class, spend time polishing
your nails, take a walk, or read a book. Take time
with yourself to upgrade your energy. Take time to
fill your cup today. What are you needing? What are
you wanting? What are you feeling? Turn inward
and do what you need to do to recharge yourself.

Ask Yourself

What is the best way I can recharge? What can I do
alone with myself? Who am I when no one is
around? What can I do that would help me to feel
whole?

June 3

Ride the current of life.

*"Sometimes you gotta just
go with the flow."*
- Old Saying

Remember

Lose yourself to new surroundings and enjoy finding yourself. Instead of fighting or forcing life into ways that wish it were, go with the flow. Ride the current that life will bring you. There is an expression: *let go of the grip you have on the shore and ride the current freely*. Travel and explore the world around you. Never lose an opportunity to see anything that is beautiful and inspiring. Take every opportunity to ride the wave of life. It might be a bit scary to do at times, but the benefits will outweigh the risk. Holding and fighting for things to go a certain way can be exhausting; sometimes, you simply have to let go and trust things will unfold in magical ways. Ask yourself what currents you can ride today?

Affirm

It's time for another adventure.
I grab new opportunities.
My adventure begins now.
I ride the current of life and go with the flow.

June 4

Give yourself attention.

"The most powerful relationship you will ever have is the relationship with yourself."
— Diane Von Furstenberg

Today's message

The greatest gift you can give yourself is a little bit of your own attention. Make time for self-care. Be good to yourself. The love and attention you always thought you wanted from someone else is the love and attention you first need to give yourself. Take time for spa-like treatments, eat healthily, do yoga or anything that makes you feel like you are caring for yourself and giving yourself the attention you deserve. There are so many benefits to taking the time to nurture and care for yourself. You have likely heard the expression: *you can't pour from an empty cup.* Take time to think about what you can do to fill up your cup today., then make time to give yourself the attention that you deserve.

Ask yourself

What would make me feel great?
How do I care for myself?
What can I do to give myself the attention I deserve?

June 5

Keep learning and growing.

"In a growth mindset, challenges are exciting rather than threatening."
- Carol Dweck

Ask yourself
How has a time of failure made me stronger? What opportunities have helped me learn and grow? How can I cherish experiences more?

Remember
Part of life's big adventure is learning and growing from experiences. Focus forward, grow from, and learn in moments you may feel broken. Life is a collection of precious moments; the trick is to learn from life, gain wisdom, and enjoy! If you are going through a struggle, it is recommended never to let struggle go to waste. Lessons will keep presenting themselves until you learn and grow from them. Take the time to reflect, be curious, and discover learning opportunities, even amongst struggles. One of the elements of well-being is accomplishment or achievement. When you learn and accomplish things in life, you contribute to your well-being. Be sure you are setting out to reach new levels of achievement today.

Affirm
Every experience is an opportunity to grow.

June 6

Think positive thoughts,
feel positive emotions.

*"Positive thoughts generate
positive feelings and attract
positive life experiences."*
- Unknown

Today's message

Your attitude determines your direction. Think positive and talk positive, and you will feel positive. Your thoughts create emotions. It is crucial to direct your thinking in a positive manner. Psychologically speaking, bad stuff weighs more than good stuff. Not only do humans tend to focus on the bad stuff, but negative things are stickier than the positive ones. It is programming to try and keep you safe. Make the excellent stuff stickier by directing your attention towards positive things and thoughts.

Remember

Train your mind to see the positive in every situation. You are the master of your mind. Try not to think about what might go wrong or what is wrong, but rather think about what might go right. Try the GLUE acronym:

G- Think about and look for the GOOD.
L- LOCATE the good feelings in your body.
U- Feel UPLIFTED by the experience.
E- EXPAND the experience by savouring.

June 7

See opportunities everywhere.

*"An enthusiastic heart
finds opportunities everywhere."*
- Paulo Coelho

Today's message

Opportunity is everywhere. The key is to make sure you develop the vision to see it. Learn also how to create opportunities for yourself. It starts with you and what you decide to put your focus and attention towards. Look with enthusiasm towards the possibilities and opportunities everywhere. Open your mind to see what is possible.

Remember

Keep building your skills and learn every day because opportunities will keep presenting themselves. The problem will arise when you overlook the options with a closed mind. Open your mind up and be creative in thinking about what could be possible. Dream to the maximum today.

Ask yourself

How can I be creative? What is possible for me? What opportunities can I jump on?

June 8

Calm your busy mind and relax.

"Your calm mind is the ultimate weapon against challenges, so relax."
-Bryant McGill

Remember

Luck is not an accident, but rather, it is meaningful synchronicity. Be open to the guidance of coincidence and pay attention. Calm your mind down by knowing everything will unfold as it will. Release the tendency to overthink. We try to control situations. Today is an excellent day to calm your mind and relax. Take a time out from thinking and overthinking. Everything happens for a reason. When you calm down your thinking, listen, and pay attention, you will see clear direction and guidance. Get calm and notice your body relax. Amazing things will happen when you let go and relax.

Affirm

If it's meant to be, it will be.
I pay attention to patterns and messages.
What is meant to be will always find its way, always.

June 9

Be disciplined with your day.

"You're not going to master the rest of your life in one day. Just relax. Master the day. Then just keep doing that every day."
- Unknown

Remember

Make note of your behaviour; be impeccable to yourself and others. Notice where you are coming up with excuses or reasons for not taking action. What do you need to do today? What is it that you want to follow through on today? If ever there was a time to shine and follow your passion, the time is right now. Maintain your power and intention to start living the life you always imagined. How can you be disciplined today? You don't have to be perfect to be excellent, be brave enough to start. Decide on a goal for yourself, and then think about the daily activities required to get you closer to that goal. Be disciplined in your days.

Affirm

I make today ridiculously amazing.
I am impeccable and take action.
I am confident and disciplined.

June 10

See yourself succeeding.

"The secret of making dreams come true
can be summarized in four c's.
They are curiosity, confidence,
courage, and constancy;
and the greatest of these is confidence."
- Walt Disney

Today's message
Never give up on a dream because it isn't happening as fast as you'd like it to happen. To accomplish anything, you need to work hard and keep dreaming big. It is common to get discouraged. Don't let great dreams die; nurse them through bad days until they become a reality for you. Have the courage to know when to let something end as well. If you have passion, grit, and perseverance, you can accomplish a lot. Adjust and recalibrate when things don't work, but don't give up on your dreams. See yourself succeeding and notice the process it might take to get you to your goals. You can do anything you set your mind to today and every day.

Remember
If you can dream it, you can do it. Dreams come to us a size too big so you can grow into them. Let your goals remain bigger than your fears. Live your dream, not someone else's. Your life will change when you put more energy into your dreams.

June 11

Open yourself up to receive.

*"Abundance is not something we acquire;
it's something we tune into."*
- Wayne Dyer

Today's message

A fantastic amount of abundance surrounds you; you simply have to start noticing and appreciating everything. Life offers you many gifts; the problem is when these gifts go unnoticed. Take time to see what you are receiving in your life already and be open to abundance for your future. Be generous, and it will become a part of your growth pattern and prosperous life. Open yourself up to the feeling of abundance. Tap into everything that you already have and all the fantastic gifts that you already possess to embody this feeling of abundance. Noticing the good in your life will open you up to receiving more of all these good things.

Ask yourself

How can I be grateful? What can I appreciate in my life? What will allow me to blossom? What makes me feel abundant and good? How can I be generous with my time, energy, and love?

June 12

You create your happiness.

"Stay calm and do what makes you happy."
- Old Saying

Today's message

You are in charge of your happiness. It is not your job to make others happy, nor will anyone else be able to make you happy. Nothing will make you happy until you choose to be happy. You create happiness with your thoughts, feelings, and actions. We often struggle and feel negative emotions mainly as a result of what we are thinking. Take notice and practice self-awareness today. Practice intentional behaviours that will contribute to your well-being. You have the choice as to how you will be today. What brings you personal happiness?

Ask yourself

What contributes to my happiness? What can I be grateful for in my life? When I was happy last? What was the thinking I had that made me feel happy? What was I doing? What was I thinking?

June 13

Be curious and open to possibilities.

"Open your hands if you want to be held."
- Rumi

Today's message
Successful people have to take significant risks knowing that they might fail. Take the steps you need to take and imagine all that is possible. Remain curious about new possibilities and open to new options. Amazing things can be birthed out of curiosity and possibility thinking. A closed mind blocks the flow of creativity. Your future is created by all the little things you do today. Lead yourself to new opportunities. Remain curious, and all kinds of interesting new things will present themselves to you. Look at things through the lens of curious child-like wonder, and you might see a new perspective. Being open is the first step to seeing possibilities.

Ask yourself
Imagine no limitations and then decide:
What do I want for myself? What can I get more curious about today? Where is my mind closed? What would I do if I could do anything? How can I be curious today?

June 14

Self-reflection.

*"Time spent in self-reflection
is never wasted; it is an intimate date
with yourself."*
- Paul TP Wong

Today's message
Take a moment to check-in and see what is going on
for you right now. Getting quiet and turning in to
your being is essential. When you turn inward, you
can self-reflect and hear your inner voice. Take
inventory of how your life is going. What needs your
attention and some adjusting at this time? The only
way you can tap into your innate knowledge is to get
quiet and reflect on yourself. Take a deep breath,
spend some time with yourself and check-in. Ask
yourself: What am I feeling? What am I needing?
What am I wanting? What is important to me right
now? No one outside of you can answer these
questions. You are your guide!

Ask yourself
What gave me the most joy today? What has
caused me inner conflict? How can I support myself
best today? What is the best way for me to check
in with myself?

June 15

Find music that lifts your spirit.

*"Music is to the soul what
words are to the mind."*
- Johnny Depp

Remember

Music is a piece of art that can be felt in the heart. Turn the music up and let your heart sing. Music is powerful because it can reorganize our brain function. Lift your emotions by selecting music that boosts your mood. Play some of your favourite songs that lift your spirits. Play it loud if you like. Dance to it and move your body. Feel the power of music in your soul today. Play soft music if you are craving peace and solitude. Music can help you process emotions too. Stomp out anger, cry out pain, flow with love, whatever you are feeling or want to feel, put some music on today. Don't be shy, move to the music. Music is a form of mindfulness and presence. It has the power to put you into a state of flow. Music can shift your mood and take you to new places in an instant.

Affirm

I enjoy music today.
Music uplifts and supports me.
I boost my mood with great music.
I let music help me express myself.

June 16

Transform.

"What you seek is seeking you."
- Rumi

Remember

Life is a blend of both positive and negative. Your reaction to situations has the power to change the situation itself. Invent the life you desire. You have the power to show up today in the way you want to be in this life. You can transform yourself in an instant. Take today to think about the person you want to be and what the best version of you looks like. You sometimes have to adjust your thinking and living to transform your life, like Thomas Manson's quote, *"You can't control the wind, but you can adjust your sails."* Transformation happens slowly over time, but you can start today to get you closer to the person you want to be tomorrow. Ask yourself: Who are you at your best? Where are you now? What do you need to do regularly to get you closer to the person you want to be? Watch the transformation begin!

Affirm

I change negatives into positives.
I am inventive with my life.
I am transforming every day.
I choose who I want to be and transform my day.

June 17

Think happy thoughts.

"Probably the biggest insight ... is that happiness is not just a place, but also a process ... Happiness is an ongoing process of fresh challenges, and ... it takes the right attitude and activities to continue to be happy."
- Ed Diener

Today's message

Think happy thoughts. When you think you're not happy with your life, know that your happiness depends on your thinking. What might be a better feeling thought? What might be a new perspective you could take that would make you feel better? It is not pretending bad things or struggles don't exist, but instead deciding how you might look at this struggle and challenge from a different lens. How can you look at things today with a compassionate and life-enhancing perspective? Most people think happiness is about gaining something, but it's not. It's all about working on your thinking and being grateful for everything you have and are in this present moment. Knowing this information makes it easier to shift to a happier place.

Ask yourself

How can I express kindness? What do I appreciate about my life? What is a better feeling thought?

June 18

Filter your world and shift your lens.

*"See the world through
rose coloured glasses."*
- Old Saying

Today's message

The world you see is created by what you focus on. It is never too late to adjust how you see the world. Your experiences and past have formed a filter through which you see the world. Sometimes we must adapt the story we might be telling ourselves. Ask yourself: How do I choose to interpret the world? What lens do I see the world through? Can I change my lens? Knowing you have the power to shift your perspective and the lens through which you see the world implies you influence your planet. Just like picking a channel to watch on TV or listen to on the radio, you have the power to choose your channel of focus and the ability to change the channel.

Affirm

I see the beauty that life has to offer.
I see the beauty within myself.
I choose to see the world as beautiful.

June 19

Good friends.

"You become like the five people you spend the most time with. Choose carefully."
- Jim Rohn

Today's message
Surround yourself with people that reflect who you want to be. Choose friends that force you to be and do better. Friends and community all have an impact on the person that you are today. Make sure you place yourself around people that influence you in a positive, uplifting manner. Make a list of the tribes, people, groups, and communities that make you feel joyful. Commit to spending more time with these groups of people or individuals. Reach out today to someone that inspires and lifts you.

Remember
Your friends should motivate and inspire you. People around you should be supportive. Quality is more important than quantity.

Ask yourself
Are my friends bringing out my best? Who are my quality friends and acquaintances? Who brings out my best? What groups do I want to be a part of?

June 20

Make good choices.

*"May your choices reflect your hopes,
not your fears."*
- Nelson Mandela

Ask yourself
What is important to me? How can I follow my own heart, live my passion, and find deep meaning? Do my choices reflect the person I wish to be?

Remember
We are all confronted with countless choices each day. The key is to honour your priorities and be brave enough to let go of what isn't working in your life. What are some excellent choices that you would like to be making? You deserve happiness. You know what you need to do. What is getting in the way of your hopes and dreams? What choices can you make today to get you closer to the person you want to be tomorrow?

Affirm
Today I am a priority.
I choose to follow my heart and make good choices.
I let go of what isn't serving me.

June 21

A lucky break is up to you.

"The harder I work, the luckier I get."
- Samuel Goldwyn

Remember

Frequently people long for the one lucky break when it comes to their career and life, forgetting that perhaps the combination of luck and hard work leads to success. If you want to do great things and be successful, it is essential to realize hard work is required. It is common to look at other's success as lucky or came easy, but what is often overlooked is the practice, failure, and determination that came before all the luck. You will have more ideas and chances in your life if you work hard and practice your craft. It is a different perspective and stage seeing the horizon when you are almost to your goal and reaching your level of success. Keep striving, working, and loving the process it takes to get you where you desire to go. After all, the harder you try, the luckier you will get.

Affirm

I work hard.
I keep practicing.
I recognize all success is a combination of hard work and luck.

June 22

Set boundaries.

*"Life is a balance of holding on
and letting go."*
- Rumi

Remember

Boundaries are a part of self-care. They are healthy and necessary. Give thanks and take nothing for granted. Balance your life with fun, laughter, and positive people. Think of boundaries as fences in your backyard. It keeps out animals and protects what is on the inside. You need to establish your boundaries. What do you value and what are your rights? Decide this and place your virtual fences so you can be protected. Be sure to compromise and respect other's boundaries well, but never give up your values, rights, and what is important to you. Make sure your compassion includes yourself. Express your boundaries clearly and confidently to those around you.

Affirm

Today, I set boundaries.
I choose to balance give and take.
I am compassionate with myself.
I protect my values and rights.

June 23

React to life positively.

*"Life is 10% what happens to us and
90% how we react to it."*
- Denis P. Kimbro

Today's message

Be mindful of how you react to things in your life. A positive mind looks for ways it can be done, and a negative mind looks for ways it cannot be done. Adopt a mindset of growth where you see the opportunities for learning and growing from what life gives you. Choose to be a hero of your life instead of a victim. You probably have heard the expression that difficult roads often lead to beautiful destinations. It isn't necessarily about fixing what is broken and challenging in your life, but rather it could be about shifting the lens with which you are looking at things.

Remember

You can deal with everything life throws at you. Choose to react as positively as you can to challenge. Look for the growth opportunity and possibilities from what life gives you. Ask yourself: What is the possible learning and opportunity to grow from this situation? How can I see this as a new opportunity? What is the good that could come out of this? If I can't see it, what can I find that I am grateful for right now?

June 24

Mindpower.

*"Your mind is everything.
What you think, you become."*
- Gautama Buddha

Remember

Your mind is very powerful. You have probably heard the expression: *whether you think you can or think you can't, either way, you are right*. You can use the power of your mind to see life through a growth mindset. Life feels calmer and more comfortable when you approach life with a mindset of opportunities. Stay curious about your life and the situations you find yourself in today. Curiosity moves you away from the tendency to judge situations and people, including yourself. Become more aware of what your mind is thinking, often it goes on automatic pilot with thoughts, judgments, and limiting beliefs. Catch your thinking. Use your mind as a powerful tool that you can shift and use to make your life better.

Affirm

I change my mind; I change my life.
My mind is powerful.
I am careful with my thoughts.
I see life through a growth mindset.
I look to live with curiosity.

June 25

One day at a time.

"Take one day at a time.
Today, after all, is the tomorrow
you worried about yesterday."
- Billy Graham

Today's message

The future can seem overwhelming and even scary, full of uncertainty. When you are worried about what the future has in store, you disrupt your peace. Try to take one day at a time. Set intentions for yourself and your future, but then detach from those intentions. The best thing about the future is that it will be coming to you one day at a time. You can handle each day. Try not to dwell on the past either, but rather take lessons and learn from the past. The present moment is the only moment that you have available to you. Try to capture the beauty in the present moment today. If you must look back, look back forgivingly. If you must look forward, do so hopefully.

Ask yourself

What makes me mindful in the present moment? What am I hopeful for in my future? What do I need to forgive or heal from my past? How can I approach each day one day at a time?

June 26

Take time for self-care
and self-compassion.

*"Self-care is how you take your power
back. Self-care is health-care"*
- Adage

Today's message

Keep focusing forward and never look back. Look back only for the lessons that you can learn from your experiences. You might need time for healing. Honour this need for being kind to yourself. Everything can heal. Open your heart to receive healing and let your heart smile. Release any burden and take action to heal yourself. Self-compassion is simply giving kindness to yourself and recognizing you are human. Be mindful and tap into your needs. Consider ways you have recovered in the past. What are some ways others heal that resonate with you? What can you do to practice healing, self-care, and compassion today?

Ask yourself

Can I take time to heal at my own pace? Do I have any wounds that need healing? Life needs me; how can I heal, grow, and focus forward?

June 27

You are lovable.

"Stay away from people who make you feel like you are hard to love."
- Unknown

Today's Message

Life is meant to be a beautiful, fun, and magical experience. Spend your time with the people who make you laugh and feel loved. Don't let other people bring you down. Stop letting people control your happiness. Be yourself and remember who you are. You are lovable. Don't think that you are not lovable, even for a second, and stay away from people that make you feel like you are hard to love. You are not hard to love. Let any haters or negative people become your motivators. You have control over whether you let someone's negative behaviours affect you. Take action to love yourself more when someone makes you feel less than lovable.

Ask Yourself

Who is trying to bring me down? What is occupying my mind right now? How can I keep calm and carry on positively? How can I love myself more today?

June 28

Focus on abundance and prosperity.

"Work harder than you think
you did yesterday."
- Alex Elle

Today's message

If you dream big, you need to work hard, stay focused, and surround yourself with good people and situations. It does not feel good to focus on lack or scarcity. Take notice of all the abundance around you and how prosperous you already are, even if it is tiny little examples of abundance and prosperity. Your effort is required to achieve great things. You can live your life at a new level; you are the only thing holding yourself back. Devote yourself to new learning and a new level of mastery. Work with all your heart. Keep your thoughts and emotions in a place of abundance and prosperity. Dwell, savour, and ruminate all about the abundance and prosperity currently in your life and watch as more unfolds.

Ask yourself

How can I start working harder than I did yesterday? What does the best version of me look like? Can I think big and act big, but most importantly, do what I love? What evidence of abundance do I see around me? What evidence of prosperity do I see around me?

June 29

Remain calm and even keel.

*"With self-discipline,
most anything is possible."*
- Theodore Roosevelt

Today's message

Take charge of how you want to run your day. Be very disciplined with yourself and do what needs to be done. Being calm and exercising self-control is not the absence of freedom, but rather it will become the source of freedom. Run your day by not letting other people, situations, and things derail you off your tracks. Decide to stay calm and even today. You are in more control when you respond rather than react. Notice places in your life and day that might benefit from calm responding instead of reacting to situations. Take a deep breath and decide to run your day today. Stay calm.

Ask yourself

How can I exercise self-control? What would make me more disciplined? How can I take action today towards my goals? What would help me stay calm in what could be stressful situations? What does it look like to respond instead of react?

June 30

Take massive action.

*"Don't dwell on what went wrong.
Instead, focus on what to do next.
Spend your energies on moving forward."*
- Denis Waitley

Today's message
Keep your head high no matter what happens. You'll be all right. Take massive action towards your dreams today. It feels good to gain momentum and take the initiative towards who you want to be. Action brings a sense of accomplishment. By doing you will feel inspired and energized. If the moment hurts, do not fall victim or dwell; learn, let go, and focus forward. Don't look in any direction but ahead. Action will move you out of a place of stale complacency.

Ask yourself
What do I need to let go? What actions, thoughts, or situations do I need to let go of? What can I move forward on? What action can I take? What needs to get started? What do I need to do to get going?

July 1

Let your spirit glow.

"Shine with all you have.
When someone tries to blow you out,
just take their oxygen and burn brighter."
- Katelyn S. Irons

Ask yourself
What people and situations dim my light? When do I feel I have lost my sparkle? Can I transform my state and look for my sparkle?

Remember
Every time you take away negative energy from your life your spirit glows brighter. Take notice of what or who is wearing you down. Without judgement around the impact it is having on you, make a change. Focus on what does make your spirit glow. Do more of what makes you sparkle with joy and happiness. Your brightness will help people who are in darkness. Make sure they are not dimming your light. We all have demons and sometimes darkness; make changes to uplift your emotional state. Take ownership and responsibility for your own brightness.

Affirm
I shine bright and my spirit glows.
I can change my state, and I choose to radiate brightness.

July 2

Be self-determined.

*"I am not what happened to me,
I am what I choose to become."*
- Carl Jung

Today's message

You have a goal that you have set for yourself. You're excited, inspired, and motivated to achieve a new level of success. The only person you are destined to become is the person that you decide to be. Even if no one believes in you and what you desire for yourself, you need to keep going. When you find yourself stalled, stuck, or stopped, tap back into your passion, energy, and grit. Remember the reasons why this is important to you. The bigger the why, the easier the how will be for you. A common coaching question is: Why do you want that? Dig deep and gain an emotional connection to all these reasons as they will keep you going when willpower or motivation dwindles. Tap into your reasons why and keep going today.

Affirm

I will be happy with who I am today.
I will keep fighting for who I desire to be tomorrow.
I am determined.
I remind myself why my goals are important and keep going.

July 3

Don't compare yourself to others.

***"Learn from everyone but
compare yourself to no one."***
- Brooke Hampton

Today's message

Stop yourself from comparing yourself to others. Try to simply see others as inspiration, not a measure of comparison, as it will deplete you and waste your energy. Focus instead on how you can keep getting better yourself. Stop comparing yourself to others because there is a never-ending feed of other people at different places in their lives. The last thing you want to do is set yourself up for failure and disappointment. Instead, it is important to look at yourself and compare yourself to who you were yesterday. How are you progressing? How can you progress today? Be aware of what triggers you to compare and avoid those situations. Remind yourself that your insecurities are natural and its normal to compare. Most people you are comparing yourself to have been practicing and working hard at what they have accomplished. Bring yourself back into your own lane and practice gratitude. Remember you are unique.

Ask Yourself

What do I want for myself? What would make me feel good about myself? What is best for me right now?

July 4

Enjoy others' beauty.

"Just because you don't look like somebody who you think is attractive doesn't mean you aren't attractive. Flowers are lovely, but so are sunsets, and they look nothing alike."
- Adage

Remember

Beauty is a funny thing. Others can be beautiful in a completely different way than you. Never let their beauty make you feel less than or inferior. Be happy for others' beauty and embrace the gift that they are. Continue to love your own beauty as well. When people tell you their good news and fortune, be genuinely happy for them. You can master the art of being happy for other people. Instead of thinking how someone else's success competes with yours, focus on how you would feel with the same fortune or situation. The positive emotions will serve you well. Make it about the other person not about your own lack. Own a bit of someone else's happiness and success and notice how good it feels. Get as enthusiastic as you can with a genuine reaction.

Affirm

I am beautiful, I am unique.
I share others' happiness.
I respond enthusiastically.

July 5

Do what is important to you.

"If it's important, you'll find a way.
If it's not, you'll find an excuse."
- Ryan Blair

Today's message

It is less about having time, and more about making time, for what is important to you. Prioritize what matters most to you. It is easy to become distracted or swayed by other people in your life, make sure you put your own priorities up high as well. You define what is important to you by what you dedicate your time to. Think about what is important for you and what you want to spend some more time on today? The first step is to get clear on what is actually important to you. What would you do if there were no obstacles in your way? What is really important to you at this time?

Ask yourself

What is the highest and best use of my time? What matters most to me? How can I be clear and prioritize what is most important to me? What distraction do I need to shift my focus away from in order to do what is important to me?

July 6

Take a break.

"Sometimes you gotta take a break from all the noise to appreciate the beauty of silence."
- Robert Tew

Remember

Just because your childhood is over, does not mean that your playtime is over. Play can make you stronger and develops your ability to laugh and see humour in life. Taking a break allows you to hit the reset button and can energize you. It is ok to close your eyes for a bit and take a rest. It is ok to step away for a while to shift your energy. Taking a break from things has the power to shift the way that you see things so that you can gain perspective. Take a break when you need it today!

Affirm

I regain perspective when I take time to recharge.
I make time for play and laughter.
My joy creates miracles.
It's ok for me to close my eyes and rest.
I recharge and come back stronger.

July 7

Create your own happy.

*"Don't let your happiness depend
on something you may lose."*
- C.S. Lewis

Today's message

You create your own happiness inside yourself. Things outside of you do not determine your happiness. You have probably heard the expression: *avoid putting the keys to your happiness in someone else's pocket*. It is such a wonderful expression that emphasizes that you have to take responsibility for your own life and happiness. No one and nothing else has the power to take that away or give it to you. Take back your power by taking ownership of your happiness. Notice all the good you already have in your life; be grateful. Shift your thinking to a place where you experience positive emotions. Practice behaviours that make you feel great. Be kind to others and be of service. Create your own happy today.

Affirm

I am in charge of my happiness.
I focus on my needs, and I fulfill them.
I choose to notice the good in my life.
I reroute negative thoughts to better feeling thoughts.
I savour the good in my life.
I act in kind ways.

July 8

Think, feel, and imagine good things.

"What you think, you become.
What you feel, you attract.
What you imagine, you create."
- Gautama Buddha

Today's message
Take notice of your thoughts. Your thinking and imagination are powerful tools you can use to bring good things into your life. Think thoughts that have a good feeling around them. Today, look for moments of joy and set your intention to savour the things that bring you joy. Think about these things and feel the feelings that go with the joy. Imagine yourself also doing things that bring you joy. Notice how thinking, feeling, and imagination can lead you to more joy. What we focus on and savour will expand.

Ask yourself
What are some good feeling thoughts? When I am joyful, what do I feel in my body? What good feelings can I experience? How can I use my imagination to create a good life for myself? What are some experiences I have been through that brought me joy?

July 9

Everything will be ok.

"What defines us is how well we rise after we fall."
- Zig Ziglar

Today's message

Pick yourself up and dry your eyes, everything will be ok. When you are feeling uncertain or overwhelmed you can tell yourself that you will be ok. You can notice how you are already safe in this moment. Take notice of how thinking you are safe and ok in this moment feels much better. Talk to yourself and calm your nervous system. There is no such thing as failing; everything is an opportunity to learn. Shift your lens from stress, overwhelm, and despair by calming your nervous system. In psychology it is called down regulating. What are you needing to feel ok in this moment?

Affirm

I can get through challenges.
It is human to not be ok at times.
I will be ok.
I am safe.
I calm myself and take a deep breath.
I have support and love around me.
I am not alone.

July 10

Making decisions.

"Every decision I make
is the right one for me."
- Louise Hay

Today's message

Will this give me energy or deplete my energy? When you're having a tough time deciding something, ask yourself this question and make a conscious choice from there. When you follow your joy and energy you will be pointed in the right direction. Often times when you are fighting or forcing something, it might not be the direction you are supposed to take. That is not to say everything will feel like butterflies and roses, but when making a decision try tweaking things and notice your level of energy and joy. That will help direct your decision. Then once you have made a decision, know that you have made the right decision for you, yourself. Do a thought experiment and go through both scenarios to see how each path makes you feel. Today, and every day, follow your energy to help make decisions.

Ask yourself

What is the best outcome for me? How will that decision make me feel? Am I considering all options? What feels energizing?

July 11

Choices and decisions.

*"I am NOT a product of my circumstances.
I am a product of my decisions."*
- Steven Covey

Today's message

Your current life is made up from the choices you have made up until today. The decisions and choices you make, even the small ones, have a compound powerful impact on the person you become. Your life is a constant stream of choices. It is important to keep making good choices and decisions. You create the world you live in with your choices. Make them good! Just like good daily decisions and choices have a profound positive impact on your health (such as the decision to walk, for example), bad decisions or habits conversely have a negative impact on your health. Who is the person you desire to be? What are the choices you need to make to get you closer to that person? You have probably heard the expression: *you are what your repeatedly do.*

Ask yourself

What are the possibilities? What good decisions can I make today? What are my choices? Who is the person I want to be?

July 12

Power of positive emotions.

"It is your responsibility to make sure that positive emotions constitute the dominating influence of your mind."
- Napoleon Hill

Today's message
Positive thoughts generate positive feelings and positive results in your life. Positive emotions build your resilience and the emotional resources needed for coping. Positive emotions will broaden your awareness, letting you see more options for problem solving and opportunities. Try to increase your positive to negative emotional ratio. Positive emotions act like nutrients. Pay more attention to and cultivate more emotions such as joy, gratitude, happiness, and serenity. Cultivate more positive emotions today. If you want to change your feelings, you can change your thoughts. Focus and ruminate about the good in your life.

Affirm
I am in charge of my feelings.
I choose good feeling thoughts.
I focus on positive emotions.
I cultivate positive emotions.

July 13

Life feels good inside with gratitude.

"Find a place inside where there's joy."
- Joseph Campbell

Today's message

Create a life that feels really good on the inside, not just that looks good on the outside to others. You need gratitude the most in hard times. Looking for the tiny, good things in every day is one of the most profound practices you can do for your health and happiness. Real beauty comes from the inside out. These tiny moments of noticing and really soaking in the goodness that each moment can bring will lift your mood, build your resilience, and make you feel good inside. Gratitude isn't about pretending bad things don't happen, but rather it is about acknowledging what is still beautiful and good, even when you are going through the toughest of days. Message someone who has touched you positively and express gratitude towards them today. Take it one breath at a time.

Ask yourself

What makes me joyful? What am I grateful for today? What do I want to bring into my life? What makes me proud of who I am? What am I grateful for even amidst struggles?

July 14

Focus on you and your inner magic.

*"Jealousy is just love and hate
at the same time."*
- Drake

Remember

Jealousy and envy are simply a lack of self-confidence and a desire for more for yourself. When you catch yourself feeling jealous or envious, think of ways you can improve your confidence and do something for yourself. Do things that work on you. Take the magic that is you and share it with the world around you. Let the energy of envy and jealousy turn into powerful motivation for yourself. Even when you don't see your magic, remember that everyone is magical in their own way. Today, share you magic with the world in some way. When you focus on you and share your magic, jealously and envy will melt away. The world needs you.

Ask yourself

What am I jealous or envious of? What is it that I would like for myself? How can I use these feelings as motivation and direction in my own life? What can I do to make myself feel better? How can I notice my strengths instead of others'? What makes me magical?

July 15

Be grateful.

"When you arise in the morning, think of what a precious privilege it is to be alive - to breathe, to think, to enjoy, to love."
- Marcus Aurelius

Today's message

Take every opportunity to marvel at all the good things in your life. When you focus on what is good and what you are grateful for in your life, it makes your world seem better. Pay attention to all the great people, the good situations, and everything that makes you smile. Put lots of attention and energy into the good things. Being grateful brings a sense of joy and peace. Every time something nice happens during your day, pause and savour the goodness in that event. Take time to look back and reflect on good things that have happened to you in the past. Look at the world around you and notice all the good in the world.

Affirm

I am surrounded by love.
I am thankful for all the blessings around me.
So many things work well for me.
I have so much to be grateful for in my life.

July 16

Value your life and be present.

*"There is so much peace
in the present moment."*
- Unknown

Remember

Your mind is a very powerful tool that you can fill with positive thoughts. Gratitude can transform your world from ordinary to a life of beauty and opportunities. It is easy to become stressed and overwhelmed. Your brain starts to translate everything it sees as a threat when you are stressed. In order to calm and halt the cycle of stress you can shift to focusing in the present moment. Take a deep breath. Take one breath at a time. Slow down. When you pump your brakes and slow down you can gain composure and things will fall back into a clear perspective. Your breath will bring you to the present moment and calm your nervous system. Be sure to be thankful and cherish each day as a gift. Move yourself to the present moment. Notice the tiny miracles all around you, even when you are thinking about your future dreams.

Affirm

There is joy in my life.
I take a deep breath and I am calming down.
I have an extraordinary life.
I value all the good things around me today.

July 17

Expect great things in this new day.

*"You must expect great things of yourself
before you can do them."*
- Michael Jordan

Today's message

Believe in yourself and expect great things; if you don't, you just might end up being right. Take the initiative to think about what great things could happen for you, what wonderful opportunities might be in store for you. It's a new day, make it as beautiful as you can. What can you do to make today extra beautiful? Try to build happiness into your day today by being present, looking for the good, saying thank you, moving your body, celebrating your accomplishments, helping others, getting outside, taking a deep breath, and reflecting on your life. Set some really fantastic dreams in place and then expect those things to show up for you. This expectation and faith will build up your strength, confidence, and motivation.

Ask yourself

What do I want most for myself? What is my desired outcome for the day? What would make my day great? What can I build into my day today?

July 18

Connect with yourself
and practice compassion.

*"The thing about truth is that
it exists beyond belief.
It is true even if nobody believes it."*
- Dieter F. Uchtdorf

Today's message

Success is about living your life according to your own truth, what is important to you. Be bold and be yourself, not what people expect you to be. You can learn a lot about yourself if you pay attention to your life. The truth will reveal itself. While going through your day be honest with yourself about what it is you desire. You define what is important to you by deciding what you spend your time doing. Practice compassion and understanding around everyone's unique desires. If humans were all the same, life would be boring. Connect to what you value, what is really important to you. Be honest with yourself and take inventory with compassion about your life.

Ask yourself

How am I genuine and original? Can I fully be myself? Where am I not being honest with myself? Am I paying attention to what inspires me in my life? What do I value? When honouring my truth how can I be compassionate at the same time?

July 19

Speak kind towards yourself.

"You will never speak to anyone more than you speak to yourself in your head, be kind to yourself."
- Unknown

Ask yourself

Am I hiding my greatness behind past guilt? Where am I striving to be perfect? What lessons keep getting presented to me? What can I learn from these situations?

Remember

Forgive and let go of the past so you control your happiness. Let go of grievance stories and position yourself as a hero. You are perfect as you are, and you are a work in progress. Remember, every day you are learning and growing. Some days you will feel like pushing and some days you will feel like resting. Be compassionate and kind with yourself. If you remove the guilt and make a commitment to yourself to learn from and do better in future situations, you take back your control. Control what you can control and decide to surrender or let go of the rest. Focus on your positive attributes and your progression. Don't be so hard on yourself.

July 20

Go for a walk or get outside.

"Thoughts come clearly while one walks."
- Thomas Mann

Today's message
Habituate yourself to walk or get outside every day. You are the most important person in your life and deserve to be taken care of. Make time for movement to increase vitality and gain perspective. When you free your body, you free your mind. Science shows us that walking improves circulation and oxygenates your entire body, mind, and spirit. Walking is a simple way to shift your perspective and change your mood. Walking can help you gain perspective and clear your mind. If you walk and talk with a friend, it will bring connection. You can walk and learn by listening to a podcast or audio book. Walk for gratitude thinking appreciative thoughts for the entire walk. Walking spurs on productivity and makes you feel energized. Life is a balance between rest and movement, get outside or go for a walk to create balance.

Ask yourself
When can I step away, get outside or take a walk? What clears my mental clutter? How can I build walking or outdoor leisure into my day today?

July 21

Be grateful and spread love.

*"The struggle ends when
gratitude begins."*
- Neale Donald Walsh

Today's message

If you're experiencing any level of emotional pain or discomfort, the easiest way to shift out of it is to ask yourself what you're grateful for. Love is a way of being in your world. Love is a choice that you can make that feels powerful. You can show up with love in every connection, interaction, and experience in your day. At times our own light goes dim and we feel down; use the power of love and gratitude to help make you shine again. Love is in how you show up and treat yourself and others. You can look at things with love and gratitude. See your day through the lens of love today. How can you love hard? Adopt love as a way of being today.

Ask yourself

What am I grateful for? How and who can I love hard today? What makes my life good? If love is a way of being, how can I be love?

July 22

Shine bright even when
you feel dull.

"Choose to shine."
- Old Saying

Today's message

Don't let anyone or anything dim your sparkle. This moment will not last forever. Believe that there are brighter days to come. Remember who you are and the light that you bring to this world. Choose to make everything around you beautiful. Create a beautiful day! Sometimes days and even months will feel tough but do remember this moment will be a memory soon. There are so many wonderful days ahead of you and coming to you. These days will be filled with so much joy, happiness, and love. Your days ahead will have fun and new adventures for you. Be strong now, knowing brighter days will come. Focus forward and keep going. One step at a time. Shine bright knowing things are coming. Brighter days lie ahead.

Affirm

I shine bright.
I am a ray of sunshine.
There are brighter days ahead.
I continue to sparkle.
This will not last forever.

July 23

Be happy and know you are enough.

"You are enough."
- Unknown

Today's Message
We are raised in a culture that makes us think that our worthiness is based upon our achievements. That only when we are successful at something will we earn our own happiness. The "I will be happy when ..." thinking. It is a cycle of thinking our worthiness is dependent on outside achievements. When we think this way, we create a cycle of the world telling us we are not good, we blame ourselves, we try to earn goodness through hard work and achievements, and if it doesn't work we feel failure - and the cycle continues. You eventually will burn out. Before you set your sights on the next big accomplishment, it is important to remember you are innately good. You don't necessarily need the next big achievement to finally be enough. You are already enough!

Affirm
I am good exactly how I am.
I do not need to earn happiness.
I do not need to be productive to be worthy.
I am good.
I am enough.

July 24

Fix what is broken.

"Make peace with your broken pieces."
- Unknown

Today's message
When something is broken you try to fix it. See your life in the same way. When you feel broken, fix yourself. If you don't know how, take time to learn and figure it out. It is ok to feel lots of feelings, good and bad. That is what it is to be human. It is normal to make mistakes, have failures, and feel broken. When you feel broken, try to embrace your different emotions and honour how you are feeling. Practice self-compassion and self-soothing. Remember that sometimes good things fall apart to make room for something better. Find space where you can support, soothe, and comfort yourself through this time. Look within and honour what might need healing.

Ask yourself
What needs my attention? What am I feeling? When I feel I'm falling apart, what helps me get back together? What can I do to make me feel good today?

July 25

Be silent and set boundaries for yourself.

"Silence isn't empty. It's full of answers."
- Lori Deschene

Today's message

Be still. Empty yourself of the mental chatter and
the busyness of life to create a state of mindfulness
and awareness. There is healing in stillness. Tap into
what you are needing. Get quiet and connect to
what boundaries you might need to set in order to
get your needs met. Remember, boundaries are for
you and your needs. The quieter your mind, the
more you hear your inner voice. Inner peace comes
when you don't let other people or events control
your emotions and thinking. You deserve to set
boundaries that assert what it is you are needing.
You deserve to set limits in order for you to be your
best. You deserve to have the space that makes you
feel good. Take time to get quiet today. Figure out
what boundaries your need to set for yourself.

Ask yourself

What am I needing? What is important to me?
What are my rights? What are some boundaries
that will support me?

July 26

Meditate and be present.

"The quieter you become,
the more you can hear."
- Baba Ram Dass

Remember

The more you meditate or reflect and spend time out in nature, the more you will raise your ability to get in touch with your inner voice. When your mind is calm you can be present in the moment. Train your mind to be in the present moment. One of the greatest gifts you can give to others is the power of being present in the moment. It is also a gift you give yourself. The practice of quieting your mind will help you give each moment care, attention, and love. Train your mind to be still. Calm your mind in the present moment. Take a deep breath to quiet the mind and bring yourself into the present moment. Practice mindfulness when you are listening to someone talk. This is a powerful way you can let someone know that they matter.

Affirm

I listen to my inner voice.
I pay close attention to my thoughts.
I choose to hear positive messages.
I am present in the moment.
I practice being mindful in the moment.

July 27

Slowly and carefully.

"A journey of a thousand miles begins with a single step."
- Lao-Tzu

Today's message

Take things slowly and carefully. Take the obstacles, or life in general, slowly and only focus on what is in front of you currently. Sometimes thinking ahead or of all the things you'd like to be doing can be overwhelming. They say don't compare someone else's middle or end to your start. Start with one step, however small that first step might be. You have to start somewhere. Keep progressing, and gradually and carefully you will get closer to what you desire. Remove urgency and overwhelm by taking one step at a time. Move from one stage to another and be sure not to measure your success by what you have achieved or measured compared to others. Plan to build habits and systems into your day that will move you closer and closer. You can keep building on the pieces of your journey towards fulfilment and accomplishment. Try to tackle everything at once, focus on one challenge at a time.

Affirm

I keep going.
I focus on what is in front of me.
Today I am one step closer than I was yesterday.
I continue to make progress.

July 28

Time to celebrate.

*"Acknowledging the good
That you already have in your life is the
foundation for all abundance."*
- Eckhart Tolle

Today's message

Be happy for all the good you have in your life and express gratitude. It is common to desire getting things and to look outward to measure your level of success. Physical things do not lead to lasting happiness. Have you caught yourself saying: *I will be happy when (you fill in the blank)*. All too often people are looking for their next level of achievement, next promotion, or next item; working hard to accomplish, achieve, and acquire, sacrificing current happiness, joy, and health. Decide today to celebrate what you already have, what you already have accomplished, and what you are already proud about. It will open the door to abundance in your life. Your abundant attitude is like a magnet that will draw positive things and people to you.

Remember

Be thankful and take time to celebrate when life is good. Be thankful and take the opportunity to grow when life is tough.

July 29

Respect your feelings as messages.

"Respect yourself enough to walk away
from anything that no longer serves you,
grows you, or makes you happy."
- Robert Tew

Today's message

Remain sensitive to parts of your life that don't make you feel good and try to remove those aspects. Pay attention to your gut feelings, whether good or bad. Limit your time with what you might call negative people. Sometimes you have to give up on or limit your exposure to certain people in your life, it simply isn't worth the struggle. Letting go is a form of honouring and respecting yourself. When we refer to others as toxic, it is a judgement. Shift to simply deciding who you choose to surround yourself with. Notice who you enjoy, and respect your feelings as indications. Let joy be your magnet. Emotional awareness helps you to know what you need and want or don't want. It helps you build better connections with yourself and others.

Ask yourself

What aspects of my life feel good? How can I protect my spirit? What people in my life raise me up?

July 30

Look up and ask good questions.

"It is not primarily our physical selves that limit us but rather our mindset about our physical limits."
- Ellen J. Langer

Today's message

Lift your head when you're down. You have to fight through some bad days to earn the best days. The questions that you ask yourself guide you to what you are looking at in that moment. The questions are powerful as to where you put your attention. You can ask better questions for more happiness and resilience. Ask yourself: What do I need to be my best self? What is most important to me right now? What are some small steps I can take today? What gives me energy and picks up my spirit? What can I control? What am I grateful for?

Affirm

I keep looking up.
I smile and look up at endless possibilities.
I keep my head up and focus on the positive.
I ask power questions.
I direct my own attention with good questions.

July 31

Be resilient.

"Resilience means you experience,
you feel, you fail, you hurt.
You fall, but you keep going."
- Andrew Zolli

Today's message

Resilience is accepting your new reality, even if it is less good than the one you had before. Adversity and suffering are part of life's teaching moments. Through them we become more resilient. If you are trying something new and struggling, remember that it is always bumpy or challenging to start. There is a process of trial and error. As you practice, learn, and grow, you will get closer to what you desire for yourself. Keep going. Hang in there. Being resilient is about failing, learning, and bouncing back. It is about building the ability to protect yourself against experiences that could be overwhelming. It also helps you restore balance in your life during difficult or stressful periods. Take care of yourself, connect with others, help others, be proactive, practice mindfulness, and keep moving towards your goals to help yourself to be more resilient.

Affirm

I am resilient and able to bounce back.
I am able to learn.
If at first it doesn't work, learn, and try again.
I have skills to help me through anything.

August 1

Choose calm.

*"Anger is a sign that something
needs to change."*
- Mark Epstein

Today's Message
Anger is a funny thing: it builds fast, and it turns off
the part of our brain that can think rationally. Anger
is a compelling emotion that can give you
motivation and energy. It can also be destructive if
not channelled effectively. Slow down, take a deep
breath, and understand that anger is a message.
What is it telling you? What needs to change?
Staying calm allows you to think logically and to
make decisions accordingly. If your mind is free and
relaxed, you can gain clarity and solutions will flow
to you. Staying calm allows you to respond instead
of reacting. Energy is everything. Be careful when
you spend your energy. Anger is a natural defence
against pain in your life, don't waste your energy
being in anger. Use this time to calm down, reflect,
and make a change. Find your Zen place.

Affirm
I am human.
I choose calm.
I am safe.
My anger is an opportunity for change.

August 2

Don't worry what people think
and take a leap.

*"If you plan on being anything less than
you are capable of being, you will probably
be unhappy all the days of your life."*
- Abraham Maslow

Today's message

Most of the time when we are interpreting what others are thinking we are not accurate. It's impossible to know what other people think. Worrying about different opinions is very draining and may not be accurate. It can even hold you back from trying new amazing things. How can you take a leap today? When you get out of your way and take that leap you have been wanting to take, you will gain a sense of accomplishment. Where have you been holding back out of fear of being judged? Each day is a new day. What intention are you setting today? What leap, big or small, will you take today?

Affirm

I choose not to read into situations.
I focus on myself.
I take leaps.
I try new things for myself.

August 3

Look for good.

*"You gotta look for the good in the bad,
the happy in the sad, the gain in your pain,
and what makes you grateful, not hateful."*
- Karen Salmansohn

Today's message

I've found that no matter how seemingly horrible a circumstance may appear, I can always find some good in it. Ask yourself, how has this happened FOR me? This shift in perception puts you instantly in a place of growth and curiosity. The growth mindset amidst challenges is an excellent tool to help you struggle well. When you hunt for the good stuff, you inevitably will see more good things in your life. In psychology, they talk about confirmation bias, where we seek to find something that will confirm our beliefs and programming. When you look for good things, you most definitely will find more good things.

Ask yourself

What good is here that I presently cannot see? What is the blessing in disguise? What is this situation telling me? Where is the good in this, big or small?

August 4

Spread happiness.

"Be the reason someone smiles today."
- Old Saying

Today's message
Compliment people. Take time to magnify their strengths, not their weaknesses. Use every opportunity to be grateful for others and express your appreciation and kindness towards them. Use your kindness and your gifts to serve others in the world. When you show up in this world with kindness, it spreads happiness. When you use your gifts to make this world better, it spreads joy. All beings deserve happiness. Make it your focus today to extend your gifts and kindness. It will not only make you feel good, but it will also have a ripple effect on the world.

Ask yourself
How can I make others smile? What actions do I make that contribute to others' happiness? Who needs my appreciation today? What gifts can I share with the world today?

August 5

Choices made today will change
your tomorrow.

*"Sometimes good things fall apart so
better things can fall together."*
-Marilyn Monroe

Today's message

It's time to wipe the slate clean and focus forward.
Sometimes you have to let go of things to make
room for new things to come into your life. Break a
pattern. Set boundaries and make changes. You
have a clean slate every day you wake up. You have
a chance to change every day. The end of something
means there is a new beginning. Choose new
thoughts. Ask for help. Switch up what you need.
The choices that seem to be small and trivial lead to
your entire future. The choices you make today can
take you on an entirely new path.

Ask yourself

What if my life needs a fresh start? What lessons
have I learned from my life so far? What new
beginning or new story do I want to write? What
tiny changes can I make today that will have a
significant impact on my future?

August 6

Notice energy levels.

"No one can make you feel inferior without your consent."
- Eleanor Roosevelt

Today's message
Think positive thoughts today and notice how your whole day will feel energized. Energy is essential to life. Your choices affect your energy levels. Everyone is unique in what builds and drains their energy. Consider the food you eat, the water your drink, the environment you are in - what affects your energy levels? Eat healthily and drink water to feel nourished and healthy today. How do thoughts or certain ways of thinking affect your energy levels? Be aware today of what energizes or drains you. Adjust your life accordingly. Choose to energize today. Be responsible for the energy you bring today.

Affirm
I feel glorious.
I am energetic.
I feel alive.
I do what feeds me more energy.

August 7

Be impeccable and take action.

"Never bend your head. Always hold it high. Look the world straight in the eye."
- Helen Keller

Today's message
Act with certainty, confidence, and positivity. Let go of doubt and hostility. One small action today can change your day. That one day can change your week. That one week can change your month. That month can change your entire year. That year can change your life! One tiny action is powerful. Now is the time to act without hesitation. Every little bit of effort makes a movement towards your goals, no matter how big or small. You were born with the ability to be outstanding and impeccable.

Ask yourself
How can I step things up a notch and gather discipline? What action can I take to reach my dreams? If plan A doesn't work, what is my next plan? What habit will have a compound effect on my life?

August 8

Pay attention to your inner
experience.

"Give yourself permission to be human."
- Tal Ben-Shahar

Remember
How someone looks on the outside is very different
at times from how they feel on the inside. Stand in
your truth, and you will walk along a path of
happiness. Make sure you listen to your voice and
be original. Behind the scenes, we experience a full
range of human emotions. We face struggle. We
experience pain. We navigate challenges. The next
time you are sharing an inner experience that is
uncomfortable, remember we are all going through
something most of the time. You are not alone. We
all have moments of discontent and feelings of
being broken at times. It is a part of being human.

Affirm
I am human.
I permit myself to be human.
I know my truth.

August 9

Appreciate those you love.

"Family: like branches on a tree
we all grow in different directions,
yet our roots remain as one."
- Old Saying

Today's message

Your roots are what has made you who you are and what you have become. Always take note of who supports you genuinely. These are the people who make up your family. When you express your appreciation for someone you will not only improve their lives but yours as well. You will feel more fulfilled because you have done something that makes someone else's life better. You will find peace when you surround yourself with caring, kind people. Never confuse people who are always around with the people that are always there for you. Your mood and daily mindset will change when you focus on positive things.

Ask yourself

What people invest in me? Who are the supportive people who can help me achieve my goals and love me without condition? Can I find ways to appreciate the people around me who love me deeply?

August 10

Spread kindness.

"Kindness makes you
the most beautiful person in the world
no matter what you look like. "
- Old Saying

Today's message

Kindness can help people that you didn't even know need your help. Be that person who makes people smile a little bigger. You never know or have the full story of others, and that is ok, but responding to people in thoughtful ways can make a difference. Kindness is contagious, so the more you offer even a bit of kindness, the more you spread it across the world. You never know what someone is dealing with. Your kindness can make a person's day, week, year, and even life.

Ask yourself

Who might need my kindness today? When was I kind, and how did it feel? What are some ways that I can practice kindness?

August 11

Everything is blossoming today.

"Be like the lotus: trust in the light, grow through the dirt, believe in new beginnings."
- Unknown

Remember

Do what you love and surround yourself with beautiful people and things. Start each day to accept yourself, live your principles, cultivate and use your gifts, help others when you can, look for the good around you, do things that bring you joy, and practice compassion for all beings. Be who you were meant to be, and blossom. If you desire love and abundance in your life, you must be willing to give away love and abundance. Your well-being and blossoming will benefit the world.

Affirm

I accept myself.
I live my principles.
I cultivate and use my gifts.
I help others when I can.
I look for the good around me.
I do things that bring me joy.
I practice compassion for all beings.

August 12

Take a negativity diet.

"Protect your enthusiasm from the
negativity of others."
- H. Jackson Brown, Jr.

Today's message

Take a negativity diet. Don't participate in any negative focus, talk, or thinking. Shift away from it as fast as you can and notice how much better your feel. Negativity is the thief of joy and enthusiasm. Don't let the setbacks colour your day. Take a pause, feel those emotions, and then keep moving forward. Avoid letting other's drama and setbacks bring you into a negative space. Acknowledge them, pause and offer compassion, then keep moving forward.

Affirm

I free myself from negative dwelling.
I speak kindly to others and myself.
I notice, pause, feel, and move forward.
I take notice of negative thoughts and emotions,
briefly hold space for them, and move to gratitude.

August 13

Drop the weight of perfection.

"Beauty is the opposite of perfection. It's confidence, charisma, and character."
- Unknown

Today's message
Being happy does not mean that everything is perfect; it means that you've decided to look beyond the imperfections. Let go of who you think you should be so that you can become who you are. What expectations are you carrying around with you? Perfection is an unattainable goal. There is nothing more beautiful than a person being unapologetically themselves, comfortable in their own imperfections. Take special notice when you are carrying around the weight of expectations. Take note of when, should you have comparisons, productivity desire, false timelines, and people people-pleasing tendencies. Decide to put down that heavy weight. Releasing that heaviness makes you feel more alive and brings out the best in you.

Ask yourself
Where am I not perfect and that it is ok? Are my goals realistic and attainable? What are the benefits of dropping the weight of imperfection?

August 14

Turn lemons into lemonade.

"Imagination will take you everywhere."
- Albert Einstein

Today's message
You create your reality with your thoughts, feelings, and attitude. The past is where you learned lessons. Be grateful for your life and apply your lessons to your future. Sometimes you need those days that are bad to truly appreciate the good days. You have probably heard the expression: *when life gives you lemons, make lemonade*. It is a reminder that you have the power to take negative challenging experiences and turn them into something positive and empowering. This phrase is used to encourage optimism, positivity, and an attitude of gratitude.

Ask yourself
How can I refocus on where I want to go? Can I think of a time that I made the best of my situation? How has the past made me better today?

August 15

Notice beautiful things.

"Life is a series of thousands of tiny miracles. Notice them."
- Unknown

Today's message
Beauty is all around you, so take the time to notice and enjoy the magnificence. There is a beauty-happiness connection. Looking at the lovely things and people in your life can improve the quality of your life. It is possible to notice beauty in the mundane. Take notice of the details and find where the beauty lies. Beauty tends to feel good, and you can find it in routine activities. Happiness can come out of very unexpected places. Savour in the cumulative positive effect that recognizing daily beauty can bring. Beauty is all around you. Take time today to open your eyes to the beauty, and you will notice and experience more beauty.

Ask yourself
What is beautiful in my life? If I were to be an outsider dropped into my life, what would they find beautiful and amazing? What is beautiful in my mundane daily activities? What will make me more aware of the beauty around me today?

August 16

Be happy for others
and rejoice with them.

*"One of the sanest, surest, and most
generous joys of life comes from being
happy over the good fortune of others."*
-Napoleon Hill

Today's message

Don't compare yourself with anyone else in this
world. Only compare yourself to the self you were
yesterday. The positive energy you exude towards
others by being happy for them will come back to
you. It feels good to be happy for others, and it
enhances your positive emotions. On some level of
when you are happy and sharing in the joy of others,
that joy is yours at that moment. Being happy for
other's happiness makes sort of like super-
happiness. Find more opportunities to rejoice with
others today.

Ask yourself

What is it about others that I can be happy for?
How can I share in another's happiness? When
good things happen to others, how can I be
enthusiastic for them? How can I remind myself
about the positivity of sharing happiness?

August 17

Imagine what is possible.

"It is what it is.
It was what it was.
It will be what it will be.
Don't stress about it."
- Unknown

Remember

Don't be afraid to try something. When you do, you can only grow. The ability to imagine things influences what you do, think, and create. Don't stress. Keep imagining what is possible for you. Do the things you love without any doubt. Don't be afraid to change. It will lead you to new beginnings and opportunities. Be curious, try new things, and ask questions. Trust means trusting in yourself, your own decisions, and your abilities. Imagination is like a sneak preview of what's to come, and it helps build trust.

Affirm

I take a risk and enjoy the rewards.
I remain curious and intrigued in my life.
I imagine great possibilities for me.
I trust in myself and my abilities.

August 18

Make your joy.

*"So plant your garden and decorate
your soul, instead of waiting
for someone to bring you flowers."*
- Jorge Luis Borges

Today's message

Do more of what brings you joy and happiness. Tap into the things that bring you joy. Take walks in nature and do things that help you reflect on what brings you joy. Making yourself happy will improve your performance and build your self-autonomy or feeling of personal influence on your life. Gaining emotional intelligence or the ability to be self-aware along with the capacity to influence your positive emotions is a powerful way to create your own happiness. Take action and personal responsibility for your own joy and happiness today. The key to happiness and joy in life is taking the responsibility to make it.

Ask yourself

How can I bring more joy and happiness into my life? What would bring me more happiness today? How can I live the highest, most genuine expression of myself?

August 19

Stand in your light.

"Keep your head high no matter what happens. You'll be alright. If the moment hurts, do not fall victim to its pain. Look ahead. Focus on what can be. Focus on dreams. You'll make it."
- Unknown

Remember

Hold your head up and feel proud; you deserve to shine. Be proud of your mini accomplishments along the way to reaching your goal. Continue to believe in yourself and stand tall. Your success can be peace of mind that you know you did your best. You did it, you have come this far; be proud. Being proud of yourself is another way of saying to yourself you have strong self-worth. When you are proud of yourself you build up your passion and belief in yourself and are grateful for your ability to show up. Being proud means you accomplished or survived something that life has thrown at you. You are inspiring and able to do great things. You are growing and learning. Be proud today.

Affirm

I am successful.
I am surrounded by victory.
I am proud of my accomplishments.

August 20

Please yourself.

"I am breaking up with people-pleasing. Is that ok?"
- Expression

Today's message
Making choices that please others is common in order to please those around us and satisfy the desire to be accepted and liked. This is hard-wired in our brains for safety. Making choices to please yourself is the key to showing up in this world using your gifts. It is not unusual to try and get others to like you. It is crucial to start enjoying yourself more. Taking care of yourself is your pathway to feeling more fulfilment and happiness. It is a gift you give to others. When your needs are met and you feel good about your life and yourself, it is easier to support and elevate others. Putting yourself first improves your happiness as well as others.

Affirm
I see beauty and light within me.
Looking after myself will help others as well.
My well-being is important.
I aim to please myself today.

August 21

Big transformations revitalize you.

"Yesterday I was clever, so I wanted to change the world. Today I am wise, so I am changing myself."
- Rumi

Today's message

There will always be change in your life. It can be scary if you only think about what you give up to make change. But change is exciting when you think about what you will gain. Keep growing and transforming. Never stop growing your human potential, and from this growth, you will gain a stronger sense of self and align with your purpose. Change is inevitable, but your transformation and growth from this change is a personal choice. With growth comes fulfillment and joy. What significant transformations can I start making today?

Affirm

I embrace change.
I am capable.
I am confident.

August 22

Enjoy the moment you are in.

"Sometimes what you're looking for comes when you're not looking at all."
- Old Saying

Today's message

Life is full of surprises and unexpected gifts. Life itself is a gift, so never forget to have fun and enjoy every moment. Living in the present moment allows you to be thankful for everything. If your happiness only stems from memories or expectations, you might be limited. When you are fully conscious of what is going on in the present moment around you. The present moment can bring you joy and happiness. The more grateful you are for your life, the more gifts will show up for you. Your life, challenges and all, is a beautiful gift filled with opportunities.

Ask yourself

How can I be thankful for what I have? What are needs of mine that are being met regularly? What gifts and opportunities, big or small, have surrounded me? How can I enjoy the present more?

August 23

Work on you.

"When you are living the best version of yourself, you inspire others."
- Dr. Steve Maraboli

Today's message
Make yourself a priority and focus on making yourself better each day. Each day is an opportunity to be a better version of yourself. Your life only gets better when you work on yourself. When you work on yourself, you can heal and transform regardless of what anyone else does. Set goals for yourself and work on them daily. When you work on yourself, you have the opportunity to free yourself from old programming, limiting beliefs, and emptiness. The path to happiness comes when you try to work hard towards a healthier, stronger, happier you. Try to understand yourself more and love yourself through the process. Working on you will breathe new life into your day!

Ask yourself
How can I love myself more today? What can I be grateful for right now? How can I be a better person today? What needs my attention and work?

August 24

Practice self-control and activation.

"You can do anything, but not everything."
- David Allen

Remember

Self-control is the ability to prevent yourself from making bad choices. Discipline your mind to remember what you desire in your life. The cost of self-control is less than the cost of lack of discipline. You can achieve great things with self-discipline. Even more important than that is the idea of activation. How can you activate yourself today? Keep in mind that your worth is entirely unrelated to where you are now and where you want to be. You are worthy of regard and love always. While practicing self-control and activation, remember to step off the achievement treadmill. While working hard towards the desired place you want to be remember that your worth is not related to your accomplishments, setbacks, or wins. Strive to see your value the entire time!

Affirm

I am in control of my life.
I am worthy and have value to offer this world.
No matter where I am or where I want to be, I am lovable.
I make good choices, self-discipline and activation move me towards the person I desire to be.
I am happy with myself right now.

August 25

Life is about choices.

"Every day brings new choices."
- Martha Beck

Today's message

When something terrible happens, you have choices: you can either let it define you or destroy you. Your life has the potential to bring you down or you can let it strengthen you. Your choices determine your character. Each person has different ideas about what is essential and what makes them feel best. Making your own choices about the things you do is very important because it gives your life meaning and alignment. Making your own choices about what is important to you helps you be more independent and in charge of your life.

Affirm

I am not what happened to me, I am what I choose to become.
Experiences make me stronger.
I make choices for myself.
I determine the direction my life goes in.

August 26

Seek progress over perfection.

*"If you're not excited about it,
it's not the right path."*
- Abraham Hicks

Today's Message

It is imperative to follow your path. Connect to the bigger picture today. Take notice of how you are progressing. Your journey is going to be unique and not a straight line. There will be ups and downs. There are no footsteps you can follow and no perfect map for you, but you can follow your joy and excitement. Start your day with behaviour changes that will support your progress. The energy you feel is a good indication of the correct path for you at any given moment. Progression in the right direction will be energizing. When you follow, your excitement, motivation, drive, and focus will be almost effortless instead of struggling and getting stressed about your future. Perfection or correct path - follow what brings you excitement! Take one task at a time and celebrate your most minor victories and biggest wins. Notice the beauty in progress.

Ask Yourself

What excites me? What is one thing I can do for myself today? What brings me joy? What am I drawn towards? How can I celebrate even the small wins?

August 27

Self-acceptance amidst failure.

*"Dear you, make peace with the mirror
and watch your reflection change."*
- Unknown

Today's message

Embrace and love yourself unconditionally. It's the most fantastic thing that you will ever own. Take care of your health and love your body for being able to house your spirit. Practicing self-acceptance helps you to realize your powerful qualities, both good and bad. When you begin to accept who you are, you set yourself up for growth and compassion. While practicing self-acceptance, you will uncover your hidden gifts and talents, and foster and grow skills you never thought possible. Value yourself regardless of accomplishment or failure. Learn from mistakes rather than allow them to bring you down. Embrace all elements of yourself. Acknowledge your strengths while also noticing any opportunity for growth in failure.

Affirm

I love myself.
I am full of love and kindness.
I am beautiful.

August 28

View yourself and your life
positively.

"My body isn't flawed; my thinking is."
- Stephanie Lahart

Today's message
Change your thinking, and you can change the way
you see yourself and the world. If you think positive
thoughts, your life and perception of yourself will be
positive. Monitor your thoughts. Most people
internalize and listen more attentively to the cruel
inner voice. The kind inner voice is not as powerful.
This inner critic comes from the high expectations
and standards that you have made for yourself. It is
almost like this inner critic or self-criticism is meant
as motivation to push through exhaustion to do
more and be more. It can lead us to depletion.
Notice where you are pushing yourself to the point
that is not comfortable. Where are you mean to
yourself to drum up motivation? Positivity and
kindness are more powerful motivators.

Ask yourself
What is the story I am telling myself about myself?
What do I hold on to that I would be better off
letting go? What are some better feeling thoughts?

August 29

Be present and trust the future
is taken care of.

*"It is in the compelling zest of high
adventure and victory and creative action
that man finds his supreme joys."*
- Antoine de Saint-Exupery

Today's message

What feels like today's limits will be tomorrow's
victories. Accept challenges so that you can feel the
power of being victorious. Keep persevering, and
outstanding accomplishments will come to you.
Perseverance means you are committed to your
goals and what you value. When you value your
goals and persevere towards them, you will intensify
your motivation level. Be present and broaden your
perspective. Gain the knowledge and skills you need
to reach your goals. Start today by finding beautiful
ways to persevere.

Ask yourself

What will help me realize how valuable I am? Am I
missing some blessings in the present moment?
What would help me forget the day's troubles and
focus on the good things? What does perseverance
mean for me today?

August 30

Take charge of your schedule.

*"If it's not useful or beautiful,
it has no place in your life."*
- Kacy Paide

Today's message
To change your life, you need to change your priorities. When you lack time, you lack in your priorities. The other factor is that what you expect of yourself in a day is different from what you can do as a human. Suffering happens when things feel unachievable. When you are not achieving results, you could feel a sense that you are not enough. Take charge of your schedule and keep moving forward towards your goals but also practice compassion and understanding. Getting organized is a daily routine that helps you finish projects that you have started. It is the first important step towards your larger goals. Take notice of your progress instead of focusing on the result.

Ask yourself
What has the highest return for my future? What stands between my dreams and me? Can I take moments every day to get more organized? What am I progressing on?

August 31

Be proud of who you are.

**"Take pride in how far you have come.
Have faith in how far you can go. But don't
forget to enjoy the journey."**
- Michael Josephson

Today's message

Don't wait until you've reached your goals to be proud of yourself. Being proud of yourself is a way of saying you have self-worth. People who are proud of themselves tend to have more passion for life, feel excited about opportunities, and are more motivated. Make sure you are proud of every step you take towards reaching your goal. Do one thing today to make you feel proud of yourself. Build yourself up and challenge negative thoughts. Identify something you are grateful for. Remind yourself that everyone has flaws, even if you can't always see them. Stand up for yourself when you have been hurt, insulted, or intimidated while still being open to constructive criticism that can help you improve yourself.

Ask yourself

What am I most proud of? Who am I when I am at my best? How would my best friend describe me? How can you turn negative thoughts into productive questions?

September 1

Love yourself.

"When I accept myself, I am freed from the burden of needing others to accept me."
- Dr. Steve Maraboli

Today's message

Other people do not determine your self-worth. You are in charge. When you love yourself, you provide a sense of security and calm to your being. When you love yourself, you are saying you are good enough and don't need validation from other people. Work on being in love with the person in the mirror. Don't limit yourself because of what people might think. Just be yourself, and let people see the real, imperfect, magical person that you are. Loving yourself is a choice you can make. Seek love, not from anyone else but yourself. Learning to love and approve of yourself is one of the hardest things to do, but it is essential. It might feel selfish at first, but then you realize that before you can genuinely love and take care of others, you need to first take care of yourself. It could be engaging in any activities that make you happy or spending time alone practicing self-care.

Affirm

I am comfortable taking care of myself.
I love me.
I am worthy of love.

September 2

Make a change where needed.

"Only I can change my life.
No one can do it for me."
- Carol Burnett

Ask yourself
Can I change something I do daily? How can I fall more in love with my decisions? What do I believe in and will take a stand about?

Remember
Every new day is a chance to be courageous and make a change. To move forward in life, you need to believe in yourself, have conviction in your beliefs, and the confidence to execute your convictions. Success means committing without any guarantee. Consider the power of seeing setbacks as an opportunity to grow and learn. What changes need to be made? See challenge as an opportunity for resilience and ask : What can I control? See suffering as an opportunity for purpose and ask: How can I help? See your dreams as an opportunity for progress and ask: What is the next step? Become more aware and make change where needed today.

Affirm
I stand up for what I believe in.
I change what needs changing.
I commit to my dreams daily.

September 3

Show up as your best self.

"Believe and act as if it were impossible to fail."
- Charles Kettering

Today's message

Today, decide how you want to be and show up in your life. Make an effort to be the person you desire to be. Act as if you are already the best version of yourself and show up exactly how you want. If you continue to show up as the best version of yourself and how you want to be, you will be impeccable. Think about the person you truly want to be. Then make every effort today to be that person. When you strive to show up in your best way, you improve because you learn new things, grow, and tap into your strengths. Along the way, you are enhancing your abilities and boosting your happiness and confidence.

Ask yourself

Who do I want to be today? What is the best version of me? What does it mean to me to be the best version of myself? What does that look like? How do I want to show up in my life today? What is one way to be impeccable today?

September 4

Live well.

"Eat like you love yourself. Move like you love yourself. Speak like you love yourself. Act like you love yourself."
- Tara Stiles

Remember

Food choices that are healthy and good for you make you feel energized and alive. Going for a walk is a beautiful way to clear your head. Make healthy choices to live well today. You deserve it. When you make good choices and live well, you feel better mentally. Regular exercise can lift your mood and help you feel better. Healthy habits lead to fewer health problems and more positive emotions. Living a healthier lifestyle means being mentally and emotionally fit. Feeling good about yourself and taking care of your health are important factors for a positive effect on every aspect of your life.

Ask yourself

How can I move my body to help energize myself? What healthy foods can I eat? How can I fuel my spirit and my body today? What great lifestyle habits can I adopt into my week?

September 5

Get some fresh air.

"Sometimes, you need to step outside, get some fresh air, and remind yourself of who you are and who you want to be."
- Unknown

Remember

Walking is the way nature intended us to move around and stay healthy. Movement is essential for the body. Movement can be like medicine because it changes a person's physical, emotional, and mental states. Step away, go for a walk, and look at life from a different perspective. The more you get fresh air, the more oxygen you will breathe in, which will increase the amount of serotonin (the happiness hormone), consequently making you feel better. Fresh air provides you with more energy and mental focus. You not only get a clearer but sharper, calmer mind, and you will feel happier and less anxious. Green space is an even bigger bonus for your mental health. Fresh air and green space have been shown scientifically to boost your immune system. Step outside, take a deep breath, and enjoy all the enhanced serotonin that is promoting a sense of happiness and well-being within you.

Affirm

I walk daily.
I enjoy fresh air and movement.
I gain a new perspective and positive outlook.

September 6

Experience stillness.

"Silence has a mysterious calming effect, allowing your soul to be at peace with your thoughts."
- Anthony Douglas Williams

Remember

How do you make time in your busy day to stop and be still? There are so many benefits to stillness. Be still and locate your inner voice. Stillness offers clarity and insight into your life. Stillness teaches us to turn inward to find happiness within. The peace you are looking for is already inside you. Be still and know that you can access this calm. You can only obtain peace from inside yourself; you will not find it in the outer world. Move past the bustle and chatter of life and listen to your inner light that guides you and feeds you.

Affirm

I find inner peace in stillness.
I move past busy chaos and choose silence.
I listen to my inner voice.
I move into stillness, where I am calm and clear.
Stillness teaches me the art of being.

September 7

Clear clutter.

"Clear clutter. Make space for you."
- Magdalena Vandenberg

Today's message

Having a clear mind and a clear space allows you to think and act with more clarity and purpose. If your space is cluttered and your mind is jammed, you don't have room for new beautiful things to enter your life. Less mess equals less stress, and that can lead to enhanced well-being. Studies have shown that not only does an uncluttered home reduce stress and increase happiness, it can also improve your habits and make you more productive. Clear your space and mind. Make room for new amazing things. Let go of unhealthy food that clutters your body as well. Everyone has some degree of clutter in their lives but taking tiny steps to clear clutter can help recharge your life.

Ask yourself

What can I do to protect my space? What clutter do I need to release? What energy is surrounding me in all my personal spaces? Where can I start to clear some clutter in my life?

September 8

Get outside and seek adventure.

"Adventure is just outside your window."
-Sadaf Zarrar

Today's message

Nature has the unique ability to restore your senses and renew your spirit. Wilderness may not be considered a luxury to many people, but it is undoubtedly necessary to renew the human spirit. There are many reasons to add adventure to your life. The positive emotions, sense of accomplishment, and flow state that come with new experiences help release stress, support mental health, and provide excitement and joy. The adventure takes you out of routine and boredom by challenging your strengths and abilities, fostering confidence and self-efficacy. Take a walk in the woods and notice you will come out of the trees much taller. You are part of the natural world - beautiful. Also, find new things to do and new adventures to try.

Ask yourself

Where can I go to connect to nature? Where can I take a walk and be in wonder about the natural beauty around me? What adventure might I try? What is something new I could do?

September 9

Trust your inner voice.

"TOLD YOU SO. Sincerely, your intuition."
- Old Saying

Today's message

The more you trust your intuition, the more empowered you become, as this provides insight and support. This voice is who you are and deserves attention. Your inner voice or intuitions are the hunches that usually help direct you and keep you safe. It helps to trust the guiding voice inside your head, your gut feeling to be heard. A healthy mind will help you take good care of yourself and make it easier to focus on good choices and direction. Intuition may not be as loud. It is that quiet voice within that exists to help guide and direct your life. Your inner voice is wise, kind, and intelligent. Some fantastic ways to tap into your inner voice today are to go for a walk or move your body, write in your journal without any filter, or choose to get curious about things.

Ask yourself

What is my inner voice telling me? Do I remember who I was before the world told me to be different? What does my intuition say before my thinking interrupts?

September 10

Accept yourself exactly as you are.

"Self-worth is not determined by others."
- Old Saying

Today's message
Try your best to accept yourself unconditionally, no matter what flaws or traits you think might exist. You are beautiful, bright, and exceptional in your own particular way. You bring unique value to this world. The problem arises when you don't believe this is true. Put a halt to those things that conspire to hold you back or bring you down. It is widespread for other people to impose their demands, beliefs, and ideas onto you. Expectations of others and seeking to please everyone are next to impossible. Choose how you want to show up and be exactly as you are and as you desire to be. Living out your expectations is a powerful way to live.

Affirm
I determine my self-worth.
I speak kindly to myself.
I keep my self-talk positive.
I hear other's perspectives. However, I turn to my expectations in the end.

September 11

Choose how you feel.

"Nobody can hurt me without my permission."
- Mahatma Gandhi

Today's message
You have a choice in every moment. Happiness is a choice and not the result of an accomplishment or desired purchase or relationship or education level. You can choose to get upset or judge, or you can choose to learn and be compassionate. You decide how things affect you with your thinking. If you want to feel better, choose a better feeling thought. No one wakes up every morning happy, nor is anyone happy all the time. Negative feelings such as sadness, disappointment, or pain are human emotions. As humans, we have the power to decide what we put our attention on in any given moment. You can, therefore, choose to focus on the positive things in your life.

Ask yourself
How can I learn from this situation? What can I think that will make me feel better? What is a better feeling thought? What am I grateful for in my life? What is good right now?

September 12

Friends make you happier.

"True friends say good things behind your back and bad things to your face."
- Unknown

Remember

Sometimes you have to let people go. Everyone in your life is meant to be there, but not all of them need to stay there until the end. Without judgment, listen to your intuition and don't waste energy on people who don't appreciate who you are. Friends contribute to our happiness and offer support and compassion. In addition to helping you cope with stress, your friends also positively influence your well-being. Being with friends and making new friends can lift your spirits and researchers have found that connections help release oxytocin in the body. This is your happiness hormone. Believe it or not, being there for your friends cheers you up as well. Savouring what is good in your friend's lives gives you a boost of positive emotions and contributes to your happiness.

Affirm

I surround myself with people that raise me up.
I choose compassion and love my friends.
I enjoy the positive people in my life.

September 13

Be kind and sweet.

*"Be kind whenever possible.
It is always possible."*
- Dalai Lama

Today's message

Exercise compassion and curiosity instead of judgment and opinions. You never know what someone might be dealing with, so exercise kindness and compassion. Researchers show that the act of helping others activates parts of the brain that makes you feel pleasure. It then releases a hormone called oxytocin. Oxytocin is the hormone that helps with social interactions and emotions. The more you are generous and kind, the more oxytocin you will release. Learning and practicing loving kindness can profoundly affect your attitude, outlook, and even your health. Practice loving kindness mediations, perform random acts of kindness, and focus on gratitude. Try thinking positive thoughts about people in your life today. Be the person that makes the world a more excellent place because of who you are inside. Tap into that place of love and care. Remember to be kind today.

Ask yourself

How can I be caring today?
What makes me a kind person?
How can I be more understanding?

September 14

Breathe in peace.

"Just breathe. You'll never live this moment again."
- Old Saying

Today's message
Just breathe: inhale positive, life-giving oxygen, and exhale tension and stress. Sometimes all you need is a breath of fresh air to oxygenate your body and mind. Deep breathing stimulates your parasympathetic nervous system, guiding the body to feel more relaxed and at peace. When you are relaxed your heart rate and blood pressure will lower and you will feel more at ease. Feel like you are inhaling love and exhaling hate, inhaling calm, exhaling chaos. All you might need is just some time to breathe. Take time to enjoy every moment of your life. Every thought and every emotion have a corresponding reaction in your breath. When you are angry, you breathe faster. When you are scared, you might hold your breath. What do you do when you have certain emotions? This means that you can change how you feel simply by changing the patterns of your breath.

Affirm
I close my eyes and take a deep breath.
I choose to relax my mind and body with my breath.
I take a deep inhalation - hold - then slowly exhale.

September 15

Be comfortable being you.

"Let your smile change the world, but don't let the world change your smile."
- Unknown

Remember

You have the freedom to be yourself. Don't let anyone or anything stand in your way of fully expressing yourself. If you are different than the people around you, don't be ashamed or worried about it. Be who you are because who you are is unique and special. When you dare to be yourself, you will be living in alignment with what you value. Being yourself is about knowing what you believe in and what you value that you can live by. Being fully yourself, you will establish your own identity that is a solid foundation no matter what life throws at you. By being yourself, you will build your courage to take your path and follow your dreams. By being yourself fully, you will find it easier to establish boundaries and set limits in your life. By being yourself, you will have a clear direction to focus on, no matter what you experience in life. Try these things to be more yourself: take a break from social media, resist the urge to please others, follow your values, get to know yourself better, and be compassionate and kind to yourself.

September 16

Surround yourself with good people.

*"You cannot expect to live a positive life if
you hang out with negative people."*
- Joel Osteen

Today's message

Be picky whom you keep around you. Associate yourself with good people of good quality. Choose people who have dreams, desires, and ambitions. If you surround yourself with positive people who build you up, the sky is the limit for you. When you surround yourself with positive people, you're more likely to adopt their beliefs, habits, and actions. Positivity and happiness are contagious. The most successful people surround themselves with happy, healthy people, and those with a positive approach to life. Surrounding yourself with people who are grateful and appreciative will increase your own positive emotions. Since you learn and grow from the people around you, you can also learn coping strategies and gain hope when you see excellent examples.

Affirm

I am kind and surround myself with kind people.
I am lovable and a good influence on others.
I am compassionate and caring.
People in my life that I associate with are kind.

September 17

Have faith in your abilities.

"Believe in yourself, and you will be unstoppable."
- Old Saying

Today's message

Stop worrying about how it's going to happen and start believing that it will. Stand firm, believe in yourself, and chase your dreams. Without humble confidence in your powers and abilities, you will not be as successful, have the ability to believe in yourself, and the potential to succeed. You need to believe in your abilities, skills, and passions to get motivated and try new things. Believing in yourself is about having faith in your ability to succeed. It's not believing you can do anything but believing that with the proper training and skills combined with passion, anything is possible for you. Start setting realistic mini goals to accomplish. Surround yourself with support and acknowledge all your accomplishments, big and small. Don't be afraid to try big things and practice in order to reach your goals. Practice self-care and self-love along the way to your dreams. Have faith. You got this.

Remember

Your wings already exist. All you need to do is FLY! Know that there is something great inside you and that you are more significant than any obstacle.

September 18

Notice what is good.

"It's so easy to look around and notice what's wrong. It takes practice to see what's right."
- Melody Beattie

Today's message
When you embrace the power of gratitude, you will notice that your ability to see beauty all around you increases. Knowing what makes you happy is being in control of your happiness. Notice the feel good answers that come from asking the question: What is good? There are a lot of myths out there about what will make you happy. The science of happiness shows that simply by asking this question, you direct your attention and thoughts to a place of good feeling. Gratitude is a powerful positive emotion. Be grateful and appreciative of all those people and things in your life. Ask yourself often that mighty question: What is good?

Remember
What you pay attention to in your life is what makes up your experience. You can choose to pay attention to all the good things that show up. It is not pretending bad things don't happen, but instead shining the spotlight where you desire it to be.

September 19

Dissolve stress and accept the things you cannot change.

"Never stress over things you can't change. The past is in the past, and it's not worth your attention."
- Old Saying

Today's message

Do you find yourself trying to change the things you have no control over? Don't stress over what you can't control. Just let it be and focus on being happy. Remember, nothing is permanent. No matter how bad the situation gets, it will change. Acceptance is the key to finding peace and happiness in the current moment. It helps you move from a place of disappointment or frustration to a place of peace and power. If you can't change a situation or an outcome, your best option is to learn how to accept it and push forward even though you wish things would be different. Try to let go of the past, find coping skills, make new meaning of or explain the situation, or set new goals for yourself to practice accepting the things you cannot change.

Affirm

I breathe in acceptance and exhale stress.
I take each day one at a time.
There is no point in me stressing when I cannot change this situation.

September 20

Stop pushing so hard.

"You are perfect exactly as you are; there is no need to change anything except the thoughts that you aren't good enough."
- Unknown

Today's message

Stop trying so hard. You are perfect how you are. Vulnerability is about not knowing if you will succeed or be defeated. It's understanding that you will sometimes succeed and sometimes fail. Stop pushing so hard when you might need a rest or a reset. Let go of who you think you are supposed to be and the goals you believe you should attain and embrace who you are right now. Ease up on yourself today. Avoid thinking so hard about everything. Stop overanalyzing and pushing due to expectations. Permit yourself to be exactly where you are right now. Tomorrow is another day. Just go. Just be, and if it feels right, just go with the flow.

Affirm

I go with the flow.
I am perfect being me.
I enjoy the flow of life.
I know when I need a rest or time to back off.

September 21

If you don't like it, change it.

"Today I have the power to change my story."
- Unknown

Today's message

Unexpected changes can happen in your life when you decide that you can take control of what you want. Change can, at times, be scary. Doing things for the first time or stepping into the unknown can be frightening. But, if you don't like something about your life, about your situation, about something you are going through, you have the power to change. It will make you happier in the end. You can make things very different. Embrace the things that you do not have control over and change the things you can. Change things that you do have control over. It takes courage to make changes and take ownership of your life. Today, look at the areas you would like to have different, take notice and ownership for the things you can change, and have the courage to try something new.

Affirm

I have the power to create change in my life.
I can change my story if I want to.
I have the power to change.
I let go of the things I cannot control.

September 22

Be a giant version of yourself.

"Sometimes, the bravest and most important thing you can do is just show up."
- Brené Brown

Remember

Victory belongs to the people that believe in it the most. Don't hide away from the true you. Be open to sharing who you are with the world. Set your goals, but then focus on the present moment full of gifts. Look to others for inspirations, not to compare or emanate, be yourself. Don't make yourself small. Be the biggest version of yourself. The world needs you and your gifts. Everyone makes the world a better place by showing up and sharing their gifts. The world needs your voice, your story, your support, your knowledge, and your wisdom. Be you and show up as a giant version of yourself with no apologies.

Affirm

Today, I focus on my blessings.
The world needs me and my gifts.
I trust good things will keep happening for me.
I make the world a better place.
The more I am myself, the more I can offer the world.

September 23

Choose harmony.

*"I believe in creating healthy habits that
nourish, not restrictions that punish."*
- Unknown

Remember

It is a beautiful thing to stay silent when someone
expects you to act out in anger. Inner peace will
begin when you choose not to allow others to
control your emotions. Inner strength and harmony
come when you make habits that build harmony in
your life. Have criteria for your thoughts and the
people around you. The requirements can be simply
asking yourself: *Have they brought me inner peace?*
Becoming more virtuous by practicing compassion,
kindness, courage, honesty, generousity and
forgivness will bring more harmony into your life.
Take actions and make choices that are good,
positive, and helpful today. Seek out opportunities
to practice these behaviours that bring harmony to
your life.

Affirm

Today, I create healthy habits.
I breathe deeply and act in virtuous ways.
I trust in harmony and find inner peace.
I am kind, honest, generous, compassionate, and
helpful.

September 24

Find strength from a challenge.

"Courage is not about having the strength to go on; it is going on when you don't have the strength."
- Teddy Roosevelt

Today's message

When everything seems dark and challenging, know that you will come out the other side stronger. It's ok to feel weak or broken at times. The struggle may come in different forms and may be given many different names such as anxiety, depression, addiction, or PTSD. According to Tedeschi and also in the positive psychology world, finding strength from challenges is an opportunity for post traumatic growth or benefit finding. It is a positive psychological change experienced because of adversity and challenges. When you see things as growth opportunities to rise to better functioning when you go through a struggle, see how it has helped you. Look for the hope that arose, the new relationships it fostered, the opportunities it brought to light. It's in these challenging moments that your strength can grow. It is during the darkest moments that we must focus hard to see the light. Stay positive by looking for the possible benefits from struggle and trust things will work out beautifully. Tomorrow is another day filled with opportunities and possibilities.

September 25

Check-in.

"Love yourself and be hopeful, because you have so much ahead of you."
- Austin Rhodes

Today's message

Take time to listen to yourself and check-in with how you are feeling or thinking. Pay attention to your thoughts and feelings. Notice when you are disappointed with yourself, when you feel lonely, when you make mistakes, when you are struggling, when you want to give up on things, when you are afraid or angry. Notice when you feel like a burden or an annoyance. Notice when your life is challenging, and do not for a second think you are not worthy. Remember to check-in and love yourself. No matter what is happening in your life right now, you are worthy. No matter how you are feeling inside. You are worthy.

Ask yourself

How am I feeling right now? How can I enjoy my life today? What is it I need today?

Affirm

I check in with myself today.
I am aware of my needs.
I listen to my inner voice.
I am worthy.

September 26

The power of yet.

"Honor the space between no longer and not yet."
- Nancy Levin

Remember

Pain and suffering are inevitable at some point in your life, but love and healing step forward to help. You may not have everything figured out and might struggle at times. The world is like a classroom. You are constantly learning and growing. According to psychologist Carol Dweck, there is one little word that has the power to inspire you to achieve incredible things. When you use the word "yet" she explains, it tells you that there is potential for growth and learning. Through practice and perseverance, we can learn new skills and progress. Next time you think you can't do something, add this tiny word to the end of your sentence. I can't juggle yet. And you will be juggling in no time.

Affirm

I may not be good at _____, yet.
I can't_____, yet.
Every one of my challenges is a hidden gift.
I am getting mentally stronger.
Through determination and deliberate practice, I can learn.

September 27

Take time to daydream.

"Imagination is more important than knowledge. For knowledge is limited, whereas imagination embraces the entire world ..."
- Albert Einstein

Today's message

Everything starts as somebody's daydream. Use your daydreams to help you imagine what your future may look like, play with options, and explore possibilities. Spend time every day visualizing another detail of your perfect future. Daydreaming is about letting your wishes and instincts play out without any obstacles. You can even troubleshoot possible barriers and figure out processes needed with daydreaming. Also, use the power of daydreaming to bring about positive emotions. When you think about people, situations, and times you love, you foster more positive emotions like joy and happiness. Keep your child-like wonder and enthusiasm alive.

Ask yourself

What fun things can I imagine and visualize? How clear am I when visualizing my dreams? When can I step away from life and connect to my child-like wonder? What can I imagine for myself? What beautiful memories can I think about?

September 28

Be open to possibilities.

"Sometimes the questions are complicated, and the answers are simple."
- Dr. Seuss

Remember

Be open to change and new opportunities. All it takes is one unique insight or idea to give you that spark of excitement, inspiration, and action. Sometimes you just have to let go, don't overthink, and simply see what happens. You will be much more powerful when you become curious and look for what is possible. When you focus on possibilities, you will have more opportunities. Thinking and being open to possibilities can help you with struggle and problem-solving. The feeling of options also broadens our minds and creativity. What is possible here? Just this question alone can make a profound difference in your day. Tomorrow is a fresh start with no mistakes in it. What feels like the end might be a new beginning.

Affirm

I am open to new beginnings.
I try new things.
Each day is a gift with new possibilities.
Opportunities are everywhere.

September 29

Face your fear and forge forward.

"The future depends on what you do today."
- Mahatma Gandhi

Today's message

Taking action may not always bring results right away, but it is the most effective way to go about creating a life you desire. Fear is a strong emotion that is designed to protect you from harm. It is normal and human to have fears, but how you deal with them can determine whether or not you reach your true potential. Vision and goals with no action will only be a dream. You have to take action to create a future you desire. You must face your fears. Otherwise, they will hold you back from reaching your goals. Wake up every day stronger and more determined than the day before. When you face your fears, the result is a burst of joy and happiness from the sense of accomplishment you gain. Break the fears down and start small. Baby steps will build your confidence in your abilities. Face a fear today.

Ask yourself

What do I have to do to get the life I desire? What are my fears? Can I define my concerns? Can I separate fact from fiction? What brings me excitement? What would I do if I wasn't afraid?

September 30

Look to joy to step away from fear.

"You have dealt with so much and done the best that you can; take a moment now to appreciate how strong you are."
- Karen Salmansohn

Today's message

There are things to be joyful about everywhere around you. You simply need to notice and pay attention to the good things in your life. There are things to be fearful about as well. Not enough time. Not the right time. Not perfect enough. Failure. No motivation. Fear plays tricks on you, making you believe that you are not capable of achieving your dreams. If you pay attention to the things that bring you joy, you will notice more things that bring you joy. Be careful what you put your attention on and choose where you focus your attention. When you seek something meaningful for yourself and might be stepping out of your comfort zone, you might experience fear. Remember, this is a good kind of fear that you are choosing for yourself. Notice the excuses that fear might be making on your behalf. Where are you being held back from your goals? When fear is present, simply point out that you are about to do something that matters to you. Where is fear holding you back? How can you step forward with joy and courage?

October 1

Follow your path.

**"Let people live their truth
without it threatening yours."**
- Brooke Hampton

Today's message
Keep moving towards your dreams. Passion is what draws you in, excites you, and propels you. Keep going towards where life is calling you to go. Following someone else's path will not lead you to happiness. Just as you have your dreams, ambitions, and hopes for the future, everyone else around you does as well. Being true to yourself is a fundamental key to achieving your take on happiness and success. Follow your path, and remember not all dreams are the same. Being happy makes you feel good, and you will feel happy when you carve out your way. Choose to be your own boss and master your own life. Keep pivoting, or course-correct your life in the direction that you desire.

Ask yourself
What is life calling of me? Which is worse: failing or never trying? What do I want most in life? What do I need to do for myself? What area of my life requires some course-correcting?

October 2

Be patient.

"Patience is passion tamed."
- Lyman Abbott

Today's message
Be patient and trust that everything is falling into place for you. Don't feel urgency or rushed. When the timing is right, it will happen. Everything falls into place. Be patient with yourself as you are transforming - practice self-compassion. Give yourself loving-kindness, acceptance, and regard as you are struggling. Know that you are human. Be mindful of your inner voice. Make sure your inner voice is kind and loving. Be patient as things transform. You need all the pieces of a puzzle to see the entire picture. You may be missing some elements of your life puzzle.

Ask yourself
How can I trust that I will be put in the right place, at the right time? If I just planted new seeds in my garden, how long would it take them to grow? How can I exercise being patient while my life buds and grows beautifully? What would a loving friend or relative say to me right now?

October 3

Transform stress.

"Stress is bad for your health if you believe it is bad for you."
- Kelly McGonigal

Today's message

Take a deep breath. Release the thought that stress is a bad thing. Stress does influence our health, but according to stress researcher Kelly McGonigal, stress is only bad for you if you believe it is terrible for you. What if you could view stress as your body getting energized and prepared to meet the challenge? What if you viewed stress as helpful? What if shifting your mindset to embrace stress as a normal part of life helps you respond to life in better ways? Overthinking and reactive stress weakens your ability to make decisions and carry them out. Life will come with ups and downs. No one is exempt from struggle or challenge. Not all stress is bad. When you see potentially stressful situations as a challenge to overcome, you can learn to stress better. Channel your energy of stress to help you and boost your performance. Notice how stress motivates you to change, reach out for help, and have more power.

Affirm

I choose to embrace stress and leverage its response to help me.
Stress is present to help me respond better.

October 4

Focus forward.

**"Don't stress the could haves.
If it had, it would have."**
- Old Saying

Remember

It is not always about fixing what is broken or not working, but rather, it is about starting over and creating something new and even better. There is sometimes a tendency to look at lost opportunities, thinking you should have, could have, or would have. This type of thinking is like going back in a time machine and wishing things could have been different. Looking at lost opportunities is about you wishing the past could have been different. See if you can look at these words in a different light. Shift the focus to the future, and see should for recommendations, the could for possibilities, and the would for imagining desired results. Making significant life changes or transitions is sometimes scary, but you won't live with any regrets. Instead of wishing the past was different, focus forward and make it what you desire.

Affirm

I am moving on.
I focus forward and make room for new.
I let go emotionally and feel lighter.
I make new opportunities for myself.

October 5

Baby steps bite size victories.

"Do something today that your future self will thank you for."
- Unknown

Today's message
We tend to forget that baby steps will keep you moving forward. Slow progress is better than no progress at all. Focus on what you can do, not on what you can't do, right now. Hard work, determination, and discipline are essential, but often overlooked are the results you can achieve from baby steps. It is common to expect big results from yourself or expect too much and become impatient. Learn to take baby steps as the simplest and most effective strategy to build confidence and reach your goals. Make one positive choice after another and look for mini victories. Break your goals into a mini, realistic, small portion of larger objectives - into bite size achievements. Keep moving forward, and as long as you're driving, you will get closer to your dreams. You will benefit from small successes as stepping stones to larger ones.

Affirm
I am getting closer to my dreams.
I take steps every day.
I believe in myself.
Even small steps every day will get me closer to my goals.

October 6

Don't worry about
what people think.

*"What you think of me
is none of my business."*
- Terry Cole-Whittaker

Today's message

Not caring what people think is the best choice you
will ever make. Don't worry about others' opinions.
Just focus on yourself and stay positive. It's essential
to know and maintain the fine line between being
inspired by others and swerving into their lane.
Remember, people who look like they live the best
and most happy life are only sharing a small portion
of their story and reality behind the scenes. Further
to that, you are the person that has to live with your
choices. It is your life, be sure to make your own
decisions. Take others' input as inspiration, then
make your own choices. Some people will always
have something to say. Allow others to give you
options to choose and consider their input but
ultimately get better at YOUR life as you go. Trust
yourself and your decisions.

Ask yourself

How can I gain control over my own life and make
my own choices and decisions?
What matters most to me?
What helps me speak my truth?

October 7

Focus on you.

"Working on myself, by myself, for myself."
- Expression

Today's message
You create your opportunities. You are entirely up to you. Cultivating joy is making lifestyle changes that will impact your life and livelihood on a day-to-day basis. Focusing on yourself will help you learn compassion and strengthen relationships. Time focused on you is a form of kindness and self-care. Your happiness makes you a better person. It is not selfish to take time to make yourself happy. When you focus on yourself, you will get more of your needs met. You will be able to handle struggles and challenge more effectively. You will be more fun to be around. You can start by making time for physical activity, eating healthily, trying mediation, writing in a journal, reading a book, spending time in nature, creating a self-care plan, or spending time doing things you love.

Ask yourself
What do I want most for myself right now? What could I do to make myself better today? What opportunities could I create for myself?

October 8

Give your cares and worries away.

*"Love is the bridge between
you and everything."*
- Rumi

Today's message

Trust that you will be ok. Take a deep breath and take care of yourself. When you feel overwhelmed and you're taking everything into your own hands, remember: the world is here to help. Everyone, at certain times in their lives, needs to take advice and receive help from others. You can cast your cares and worries on to those who love and care about you. Worry and uneasy feelings are a part of humanity. It is common to feel overwhelmed at times. Worry is the opposite of faith. It can steal peace and wear you down. At times you might need to cast your cares and worries away. Humble yourself and ask for help. You can pray, reach out, or connect with others to help raise you up when you are knocked down.

Affirm

I have faith things will work out for me.
I give my worries and cares away.
I accept support and help from others.
I release my worry and move towards faith.

October 9

Expect good things and good luck.

"Just because the past didn't turn out like you wanted it to doesn't mean your future can't be better than you ever imagined."
- Ziad K. Abdelnour

Today's message

People will change in your life, things will go wrong, bad situations will happen, but life goes on. You must move on and trust that everything happens for a reason - that in the end, it's for the best, and you will be ok. When bad things happen, don't let the situation define you or destroy you. Let it strengthen you. Shift your mindset towards feeling lucky. Your attitude towards luck might influence how happy you are. Recent studies have shown that happy people have particular beliefs about luck. They're less likely to see luck as an outer force that makes things happen for people, and more likely to consider themselves personally lucky. When you think you are fortunate, you tend to gain personal agency and self-determination, which leads to more motivation to pursue goals, take risks, and learn and grow from mistakes, which ironically makes people more "lucky." One way to start developing luck thinking is to notice the good things and fortune in your life as they happen.

October 10

Add and subtract from your life.

"Less stuff. More Space.
Less stress. More life."
- Unknown

Today's message

Access what needs to be added into your life that you might be lacking and decide what needs to be taken out of your life Happiness is a game of subtraction and addition: adding more joy and enhancing positive emotions and removing or letting go of things that cause negative emotions that may be getting in the way. More isn't always better for you in life. Life is commonly full of distraction, the hustle and bustle. Sometimes removing yourself from the world and simplifying your life can seem impossible. Sometimes less is more when it comes to your happiness. See where you can subtract from your life. Clutter leads to anxiety and stress, which is why simplifying and removing becomes essential for our happiness. Time is valuable. Make great use of your time by eliminating time wasters. Surround yourself with people you love. By simplifying your life, you can become calmer and more joyful in the present moment.

Ask yourself

What's missing in my life? What is cluttering my life? How can I bring more joy into my life?

October 11

Purify your thoughts.

"Never organize what you can discard."
- Unknown

Remember

Declutter your life and feel a sense of purification. Have nothing in your house that you do not find helpful or believe is beautiful. Take this to the next level and purify your thoughts and thinking. Notice all the things that are weighing you down. Not just things, but also habits, thoughts, or people. Get rid of all that clutter. The more you can let go, the lighter you will feel. Be mindful and virtuous. Access peace and solitude. Put on some beautiful music. Walk outside. Tidy up. The mind is a powerful mechanism. Take time to watch your mind and what you're thinking. Shape your thinking into pure thoughts. Thoughts that bring you joy. Thoughts create a flow of peace inside you. Halt, stop, or shift thoughts that are restless, disturbing, or impure. Relax your mind and purify your thoughts today. Be mindful and aware of your thinking today.

Affirm

I let go of clutter and impure thoughts.
I cleanse my space and declutter my mind.
I purify my thoughts towards positive, peaceful thoughts.

October 12

Take a break, gain perspective.

"It is ok to take a break."
- Unknown

Remember

Balance, peace, and joy are all states that allow you to gain a positive perspective on your life. Take time to be still and relax. It is not selfish to love and care for yourself. Find ways to pamper yourself and make your happiness a priority. Taking a break helps relax your mind and clear your head. While you give yourself permission to relax and take some time to do something different, you can gain a different, sometimes clearer perspective. Whether it is simply taking a 20-minute replenishing nap, a daily walk, or a getaway, you are not too busy to take breaks. A break prevents you from getting bored and losing your focus. In science, they call it deactivating your goals at times to break up your long tasks. Taking a break can also help you re-evaluate your goals by gaining a new perspective.

Affirm

I am having a little me time.
I am balanced and pampered.
I am peaceful and take time to relax.

October 13

New day.

"Each morning, we are born again.
What we do today is what matters most."
- Gautama Buddha

Today's message

It's a fresh new day, with new energy and new opportunities. Start your day with a fresh thankful mind. Rise and shine bright throughout your day. See today as a beautiful opportunity to start fresh and positively. See you today with renewed spirit. Being appreciative about each new day allows you to reflect on the beauty, gifts, and opportunities that every day can bring. It gives you a jolt of renewed energy and a fresh perspective. When you begin your day, start by using an affirmation that encourages you to see the day as a fresh new day filled with possibilities.

Affirm

It's a great day to have a great day.
I am excited about what today will bring.
It's a fresh start today.
Today is a fresh start for me, filled with opportunities.

October 14

Self-acceptance and self-love.

"Awakening self-acceptance makes space for inner peace."
- Old Saying

Ask yourself
What makes me who I am? When was the last time I was proud of myself? Why?

Today's message
Growth begins when you start accepting yourself for who you are today. It is common to set high standards and be pushed by the idea of perfection. Today is a great day to accept the person that you have become fully. You don't always give yourself credit for the lives you have touched or for the person you are becoming. It is common to forget that everyone has flaws, including the people you perceive as perfect and successful. Remember that you are a special gift to this world. Loving and accepting yourself brings a beautiful sense of peace and tranquillity. Self-love and self-acceptance are critical aspects of health and happiness. Today, focus on yourself instead of looking at other people. Get rid of the need to change something about you.

Affirm
I approve of myself, I love myself.
I am unique and beautiful.

October 15

Give yourself some space.

*"Peace is the result of retraining
your mind to process life as it is, rather
than as you think it should be."*
- Dr. Wayne W. Dyer

Remember

Next time you are exhausted, take a step back. You need to give yourself more love and affection. Be kind to yourself. You are unique and good enough. Ease up and be nice to yourself. Life can be complicated and challenging at times. See things as they are and be ok with that. Being alone does not have to be lonely. Taking some space allows you to restore yourself. Life can get busy and full; it becomes essential to take some time and space to yourself. Everyone needs personal space in all forms, including relationships, workspace, or even in your own home. Personal space can be in the form of both mental and physical. Today, take some space, whether it be mentally or physically. Step away and notice how you feel as a result.

Affirm

I ease up on myself and take some space.
I take breathing space to refresh my spirit.
I am kind to myself and claim some much-needed space.

October 16

Fill your life with positive energy.

"Positive energy attracts positive energy."
- Micheal J. Tamura

Today's message

Developing and maintaining more positive energy requires more than just thinking happy thoughts. Positive energy is about anticipating good, expecting good, and believing that things will work out favourably in the end. You put off an energy field that affects the world around you. Work on keeping your energy positive and balanced. Clear away toxic, negative thoughts from your thinking. Shift your attitude to a place that feels positive and expects good things to happen. You can cultivate positive energy every day. Positivity is something you can work on and get better at through practice. The first step is to be aware when you have negative thoughts and emotions, honour those feelings. Find blessings and lessons in any situation. Avoid speaking about problems, illnesses, worries or gossiping. Discuss ideas, excitement, opportunities, and joyful experiences instead. Be grateful.

Ask yourself

Do I need to adjust my thinking? Can I grow thoughts in my mind that will produce a beautiful bouquet?

October 17

Be on your team.

"Work on being in love with the person in the mirror who has been through so much but is still standing."
- Unknown

Today's message

Be confident in who you are. You are unique, beautiful, and the only person on this earth like you. Notice your talents, your skills, and your natural abilities. Self-love is critical for happiness in your life. Self-love is defined as deliberately acting in a manner that provides care and compassion for yourself. It is much more than simply a day at the spa or a bubble bath. To truly practice self-love, you need to have high regard for your well-being. Self-love and being on your team is about trusting yourself, asserting your boundaries, and fostering a deep connection with the person you are today. Make sure you are talking kindly towards yourself and making yourself a priority. Tap into what you value and make the time and a place for all the things you love.

Ask yourself

How can I cheer myself on? What would my cheerleader say? What are my character strengths? How can I act compassionately towards myself?

October 18

Take time for inner reflection.

"Do not look for a sanctuary in anyone except yourself."
- Wolfgang Mozart

Today's message
Go within every day, and you will find inner strength as you listen to your guidance, voice, and intuition. Self-reflection allows you to look back and see where you have come so far, where you are now, as well as where you'd like to be. Returning to a place of solitude is stillness. When you go within and connect with your true self, you realize true strength. Listen to your inner voice and follow it because it is who you are. When you can check in with yourself, you will gain self-awareness. Allow yourself to look neutrally at your thoughts, feelings, emotions, and actions. Take time to write down a few thoughts about your day today. Check-in and make time for inner self-reflection. The moment you pause amidst chaos, busyness, and life in general, is the moment you find peace and opportunity.

Ask yourself
How can I shut out the world and go within? How can I become a little wiser every day simply by observing? My inner voice is who I am: what is it saying? What am I thinking, feeling, wanting, needing?

October 19

Simplify your life and open space.

"The hardest thing in the world to do is to simplify your life; it's so easy to make it complex."
- Yvon Chouinard

Remember

Simplicity is uncomplicated and straightforward. Life can be complicated if we make it that way. Life becomes lighter and brighter when you focus on what truly matters. Rid yourself of clutter, both mentally and physically, to keep peace and calm in your life. Simplifying can lead to more time, less stress, more health, and a greater chance of well-being. Simplify your life by getting rid of anything that is no longer serving you. Open extra space for things, events, people, and thoughts that bring you joy and pleasure. Simple living and minimalism go hand and hand. To simplify, decide your priorities, learn to say no, limit distractions, focus on acting on what is important to you, make tasks that are aligned with your preferences, evaluate your habits, simplify your space daily, automate some systems, learn how to become organized, journal to declutter your mind, surround yourself with people who add value to your life, and simplify your goals.

Affirm

I simplify and declutter my life.
I feel calm and focus on what matters most.

October 20

Observe and stay curious
without judgement.

*"When you judge another, you do not
define them. You define yourself."*
- Wayne Dyer

Remember

Let the power of love and peace overpower any
struggle or judgment. Instead of letting people pull
you into drama or tension, pull them into your
peace. Let your joy, love, and beauty rise to the
surface. Keep in mind that judgements are
assumptions and not necessarily the truth. Being
judgemental does not feel good, and it brings more
negative emotions. It is easy to become judgmental
and harshly critical of others and of yourself. When
you stay in a place of curiosity and observation, you
will naturally be more compassionate. Compassion
brings about positive emotion leading to more
happiness. It is about being able to see the
situations, people, and things as they are instead of
seeing them how you think they should be. Today,
don't judge. Stay curious.

Ask yourself

How can I fill my mind with non-judgmental
thinking? How can I see and listen with love? How
can I get more curious and simply observe?

October 21

Trust and be open.

"Old ways won't open new doors."
- Old Saying

Remember

When you are open and willing to receive support and love, the universe will open doors and hands to you. Letting go and trusting gives you freedom, and freedom is one of the conditions contributing to happiness. Have faith in your journey and in the fact that everything had to happen precisely as it has in order to guide you in the right direction. See the light in your heart and all the people around you. Believe in yourself and others. Open hearts build up lives and foster positive emotions. To build trust and be more relaxed, try to meditate and look for evidence of how life forms many blessings. Use gratitude to allow you to open up to this kind of thinking. Building trust requires that you be open to allowing. Try to judge less and accept more of yourself and the truths of those around you. Let go of unrealistic expectations and control. Influence your life with open hands and heart. Delve into your spiritual practice to help you open yourself up to life.

Ask yourself

Am I using up my energy with worry and fear? How can I be more open and trust in my life? How can I have more faith?

October 22

Focus on what is great.

*"Keep your face always toward
the sunshine, and shadows
will fall behind you."*
- Walt Whitman

Remember

Pain is an inevitable part of life, but the suffering that comes from holding onto the pain too long is optional. Shift your perception to focus on good things in your life. Be strong because things will get better. Happiness is essential, and science confirms that happier people are more successful, have better relationships, have less stress, live longer, are more creative, healthier, and more generous. Bringing more happiness into your life has far more benefits than simply feeling good. When you focus more on positive things and reduce focusing on negative things, you experience a higher happiness ratio. Negative thoughts cause your brain to respond with emotions like sadness, anger, and frustration. Conversely, positive focus and thoughts cause the brain to respond with emotions like joy and happiness.

Affirm

Today, I take notice of all the good things in my life.
I focus on what is good.
I let go of what isn't working and shift my focus.

October 23

Connect to what inspires you.

"Never give up on something that you can't go a day without thinking about."
- Winston Churchill

Today's message

Discipline is doing what needs to be done. Even on those days you don't feel like doing it. Never give up on your dreams. Inspiration matters in your life. Pleasure, comfort, gratitude, hope, and inspiration are examples of positive emotions. Inspiration may sometimes be overlooked. Inspiration can provide a positive effect when going after big goals. Let go of any fears that prevent you from achieving your life desires. Let your inspiration be a compass. Reactivate your dreams regularly and connect to your source of energy. What brings you energy and inspires you? Inspiration brings you motivation to pursue goals, be creative, and enhance your life.

Ask yourself

What makes me excited? What do I do when no one is watching? What brings me energy? What inspires me? Who inspires me? What does this inspiration tell me?

October 24

Honour your beauty, love your soul.

"Be your kind of beautiful."
- Marilyn Monroe

Today's message

You are one of a kind. There is no chance of a replica. Beauty is more profound than just your face and your body; it is the light in your heart. Intimate relationships are one form of a relationship that can enrich your life. It is equalling, if not more important, to love yourself first. As you love yourself first, you will be able to know what you deserve and what you are worthy of in your life. Be kind to yourself through emotional pain, life hurts, and shortcomings. Feel love within you and be loving towards yourself. Embrace yourself and be grateful as needed today. Give yourself to others in service and notice your beauty and kindness shine through. Seek grace and beauty in all the people around you, and you will find it will also become who you are. You are beautiful, and not one person, image, or comment has the right to make you feel like you are not attractive. Learn to be compassionate with yourself.

Ask yourself

How can I concentrate on finding my inner beauty, my inner love, and my inner joy? What do I like about myself? What are the things in my life that are beautiful?

October 25

Explore new ways.

"Sometimes, you find yourself in the middle of nowhere, and sometimes, in the middle of nowhere, you find yourself."
- Stacy Westfall

Today's message

Be brave enough to explore, grow, and break free. If you want to fly, you need to break away from the things that weigh you down. Novelty is an essential element that makes life exciting. Well-being researchers have identified that humans desire to have novel experiences called neophilia. People who actively seek out new experiences throughout life live happier, healthier lives. Novelty and change release the reward chemical in your body called dopamine. If you explore, you will discover yourself and collect new exciting moments. Put away your phone and enjoy the world differently today. Switch up your routines and schedule. Listen to new music or take a different drive home. Do some exploring or try a new sport. Explore new possibilities for yourself and watch your world open up to you.

Ask yourself

Is my routine mundane? What can I do differently?

October 26

Let goals keep you on track.

*"Don't be pushed by your problems.
Be led by your dreams."*
- Ralph Waldo Emmerson

Today's message

Stay focused on your goals and picture the results to have a clear image of what you can achieve. Put your attention on the things that you would like to accomplish. Don't compare yourself to others. Stay focused on your journey and ignore the "noise." It is important to let your personal goals keep you on track. Feeling good about the future and looking at the process you will take to get to it is vital for your happiness. Mini accomplishments and daily movement towards a bigger goal are very motivating. Goals help to motivate and excite you in the day-to-day. Choosing ambitious yet achievable goals will give your life direction, focus, and a sense of accomplishment. One of the elements of well-being is a sense of accomplishment.

Ask yourself

What goals have I set for myself? Do my goals need adjusting? What is my top priority right now? Can I break down my goals into sub-goals or action tasks?

October 27

Seek support and gain harmony.

*"Family is a life jacket in
the stormy sea of life."*
- J. K. Rowling

Remember

Family isn't always about the people in your life that are blood relations; it's about the people in your life who want you in it. It is important to surround yourself with family and friends that can support and comfort you in both times of joy and distress. When you are going through a challenge, a supportive relationship is vital to your resilience and well-being. When things are great, they are just the people to talk to and spread positive emotions. Family and friends will also need your support at times, and offering kindness grows positive emotions. These people support, love, and choose to align with you. Find peace, strength, and harmony in knowing you have people who know you well and support you unconditionally. Other people matter in your life. Who can you reach out to today?

Affirm

I appreciate my family and my roots.
I surround myself with people who care.
I love those around me.
I am a good friend and support.
I reach out to others.

October 28

Effective energy flow.

"Everything around us is made up of energy. To attract positive things in your life, start by giving off positive energy."
- Ralph Waldo Emerson

Today's message

You have probably heard the expression and rhyme: *where attention goes energy flows*. You are the most important person in your life, so be sure to take time every day to restore your vitality and energy. Take notice of where your attention is going. Be cautious where your energy is flowing to. Once you place your attention on something, know that energy will flow in that direction. Ask yourself where you want to focus your attention and where you want your energy to go. People can inspire you, or they can drain you. Focus on what excites you and fires your passion. Allow positive energy to flow through you and the things you want to grow and foster in your life. Move away from placing your attention on things that don't deserve your energy. Be picky as to what gets to have your attention and energy.

Ask yourself

What am I focusing on, and what is getting my attention? Where is my energy flowing?

October 29

Positive changes and healing.

"Your life does not get better by chance.
It gets better by change."
- Jim Rohn

Today's message

Life has a funny way of working out, just when you start to believe it isn't going as planned. Everything in your life reflects the choices that you have made. Healing is crucial for your health and well-being. You don't have to wait for the perfect day to start healing and feeling better. You can have joy today. Happiness and joy can even help you heal, and they are available to you at any moment. It is not about pretending bad things have not happened, but instead taking the time to lick your wounds and experience joy again. Let yourself grieve, take care of yourself, pamper yourself, get physical, take some peaceful solitude, be of service to others, get back up on your feet again. You will bounce back from setbacks as you train yourself to spend less time worrying and more time happy. Hiccups don't have to set you back for long. Reach out for support if you need it and stay committed and engaged in your life as you heal.

Remember

Sometimes you need to be alone and heal. Take time to look at where you have been and where you want to go. Transform your hurt to healing.

October 30

Complete tasks.

"The day she let go of the things that were weighing her down was the day she began to shine the brightest."
- Katrina Mayer

Remember

Organize your life around your passion, and don't put things off until tomorrow if you can do them today. Productivity is important when it comes to being happy. Productivity brings focus, meaning, and purpose, whereas busyness brings stress. Sometimes procrastination can weigh us down. There is an expression that emphasizes finishing projects: *Don't stop when you are tired. You can stop when you are done.* Finishing projects and tasks is energizing and brings positive emotions like joy. Productivity and happiness are closely linked. Completing tasks brings a powerful sense of accomplishment and fulfilment. Taking charge of your schedule is a part of taking control of your life. Checking things off your tasks list, working towards a goal, picking up loose ends, doing what you set out to do, and having a purpose to strive for all bring about positive emotions such as happiness and joy.

Affirm

I run my day and my schedule.
I am motivated and organized.
I take control of clutter and organize my life.

October 31

Be present and mindful.

"The most precious gift we can offer others
Is our presence. When mindfulness
embraces those we love,
they will bloom like flowers."
- Thich Nhat Hanh

Remember

Life brings many turns and twists. Life can become busy, full, and affected by pressure. It is easy to go into autopilot mode and miss many blessings and moments in life. Dream passionately and remain grateful for all the gifts around you. Being mindful has been shown to help us be healthier, less affected by stress, more relaxed, more creative, more open to learning, and deepens relationships. Abundance follows gratitude. Gratitude comes from being mindful in the moment of all the gifts around you and inside you. The more you appreciate, the more you will be perceptive to the abundance in your life. Be present and mindful of your thoughts and experiences. Being mindful helps you to stop worrying about your future, let go of the past, and have a more fulfilling life in the present moment.

Affirm

I am mindful and full of gratitude.
Opportunities are surrounding me.
I notice all the gifts around me.

November 1

Follow what is important to you.

"The cost of not following your heart is spending the rest of your life wishing you had."
- Unknown

Today's message

Trust what you love and continue to do the things that are important to you. Do them often. By following your passion and by doing what is important to you, your path will become clear. When you follow your heart and what is important to you, you will be on a course of authentic direction. Your life will flow with ease and feel "right" when you stay true to what is important to you. Going along with your heart and what is essential to you brings out your passion, joy, excitement, curiosity, playfulness, adventure and fulfilment. Choose your truth every day.

Ask yourself

What is most important to me? How can I build my life around what is important to me? What would I do if I put myself on the top of my to-do list today? What is my heart telling me?

November 2

Be caring and kind.

*"Even after all this time, the Sun never says
to the Earth, 'You owe me.' Look what
happens with love like that.
It lights the whole sky."*
- Hāfiz

Remember

Unconditional love is a beautiful gift that you can
give to others and that you can receive. Be sure not
to expect people to understand you fully, but do
expect them to accept and love you unconditionally.
Being able to be patient and caring in your
relationships will help bring relationship harmony.
Your well-being and happiness have an impact on
those around you. Volunteering your time or energy
to help others makes the world a better place, and
it also makes you better. Studies indicate that the
very act of being kind and giving back to others can
boost your happiness, health, and sense of well-
being. Offer kindness by paying attention to people
around you. What can you do to make someone's
life easier? Volunteer your time and energy for
others. Donate to a cause or offer care to those who
need it - express gratitude to those around you.

Ask yourself

Am I loving towards others? Am I loving in general?
How can I remain non-judgmental?

November 3

Step beyond your limitations.

*"Freedom is being you without
anyone's permission."*
- Steven Goad

Today's message
Freedom is when you realize that you can do absolutely anything. Accept that you were born to be great. Express yourself and don't mind what other people say or think about you. Decide once and for all that you deserve to have an extraordinary life and that you are unique. There is power in believing that you can do anything; with practice, you can improve. Practice does not make you perfect, but it does make you progress and get better at things. When challenges arise, adopt a mindset of possibility and growth. As Carol Dweck's work on mindset demonstrates, there is power in believing you can improve and adding the phrase "not yet."

Ask yourself
What am I holding back from? What would I do if I wasn't afraid? What can't I do yet? What do I want to learn and improve upon? What is a different way to look at this limitation?

November 4

Clear your space.

"Clutter is not just physical stuff. It's old ideas, toxic relationships, and bad habits. Clutter is anything that does not support your better self."
- Eleanor Brown

Remember

Take notice of your environment. Clear your head by clearing your space. According to Feng Shui, when you throw out the physical clutter, you clear your mind, and when you throw out the mental clutter, you clear your soul. Choose light, healthy foods for your body, and de-clutter even your diet. Let go of old habits that are no longer serving you well. Ask yourself: Is this strengthening me as a person or teaching me something? Let go of the things that are holding you back from greatness in your life. Loosen your grip on old habits that don't positively help you. It's time to let go of those unhealthy relationships and start making space for a community of support and positivity.

Affirm

I clear my space and fill it with people and things that will support me.
I shift my energy and clear my space.
I release anything not serving me.
I add only things that positively serve me.

November 5

Restriction might be in your mind.

*"Challenge your self-limiting beliefs.
Most of them are not true at all."*
- Old Saying

Today's message
Sometimes your biggest bully and your most significant challenge is yourself. Don't limit yourself to what you think you can't do; push further and think about what you *can* do. Limiting beliefs can have a negative effect on your life and have the potential to hold you back from amazing things. The only limits in your life are the ones that you create with your mind. It is time to let go of these false beliefs that prevent you from pursuing your goals and desires. Your beliefs can put boundaries or limitations on what you believe is possible for you. Challenge your limiting beliefs by asking a few of the following questions. Keep striving professionally and personally in your life. Challenge the story that you keep telling yourself. What you tell yourself is what you believe.

Ask yourself
What if I'm wrong? How is this belief serving me? How can I create an alternative belief? Looking at options, what can I do?

November 6

Move in the direction of
your dreams.

*"Set a goal that makes you want to jump
out of bed in the morning."*
- Brian Tracy

Today's message

You were born to be a winner, but you need to prepare and expect to win in order to be that winner. Good things come to those who embrace their heart's desire and go after their dreams. Your dreams can give you purpose and focus in life. Even if your goals feel unattainable at times, they are essential to keep you goal-oriented and fuel your motivation. At times, it is common to get stuck in a rut and feel unmotivated. Let your dreams be your goals. Stop waiting and start doing it, now is the time. Take full responsibility for your life, move forward in the direction you desire. By moving in the direction of your dreams, your life will feel like you are in motion. Determination, action, and faith will be ignited if you keep taking steps towards your dreams every day.

Affirm

I follow my dreams daily.
I am capable.
I take baby steps every day.

November 7

Have a confident mindset.

"Confidence is not 'They will like me.'
Confidence is 'I'll be fine if they don't.'"
- Christina Grimme

Today's message

What you think of yourself is much more important than what people think of you. Have confidence in yourself. Confident people have a different mindset when it comes to failure. When you feel self-assured you can view failures as temporary setbacks and opportunities. It is also important not to judge yourself harshly and view yourself as a disappointment. Keep your level of self-worth up even amongst let down. Don't second-guess who you are. Be nice to yourself and listen to the voice inside your head; make sure it is kind and encouraging. Remember that no one is perfect and look at failure as a temporary setback that you can navigate. Focus on the skills you can develop and what you can change. Celebrate all your victories, even the small ones. See your self-worth or value that you bring to this world.

Ask yourself

When did I last feel confident? Why? What value do I bring to the world? What would someone who loves me say about me? How can I believe in myself more?

November 8

Find inspiration and mentors.

"Wanting to be someone else is a waste of the person that you are."
- Marilyn Monroe

Today's message

When you catch yourself comparing yourself to others and wishing you were more like someone else, stop yourself. A mentor is someone who allows you to see what is possible, and this ignites hope inside of yourself. Foster and develop relationships with people who can share knowledge, experience, and advice with you. Find people that see your potential and will push you to be great. Look to others as an opportunity for inspiration and influence to make yourself better and more uniquely you. Find partnerships with people like coaches, trainers, or consultants that can help you learn and grow. Mentors and people of inspiration can help you to: build your skills, gain perspective, learn new ways of being, develop hope and faith, and to advance your career or life.

Remember

Stay true to who you are and view others to be an inspiration and an opportunity to be creative to add to the great person you already are. Be who you are while gaining valuable advice, develop your skills, gain perspective, and harness hope.

November 9

Stop self-criticism.

"Be kind to yourself; you are amazing, you are good enough, and you are worthy."
- Elizabeth Gaskell

Today's message

Open your heart. Your private inner dialogue can either be empowering or destructive. Loving yourself means acceptance, kindness, and genuine self-care. Sometimes people think that being hard on yourself will motivate change. If you have been criticizing yourself for a long time, take notice, try approving of yourself, and see how it makes you feel. Self-compassion leads to increased strength, positive emotions, and is much more motivating. When you are kind towards yourself, you are more likely to embrace challenges and improve your performance in your life. Prevent the defeating effects of self-criticism by practicing self-compassion. Notice how self-compassion allows for peace, love, and acceptance to thrive. Take action today to remove any doubt and stop any self-criticism that you might have. Play devil's advocate with your self-critic or change the channel to another inner nurturer voice.

Affirm

I speak kindly to myself.
I open my heart to self-kindness.
I love myself.

November 10

Be strong and use your strengths.

"Strength doesn't come from what you can do. It comes from overcoming the things you once thought you couldn't."
- Rikki Rogers

Today's message

Stand up for what you believe in and what is true for you. Keep your head up and face what you need to face. Tap into how you have shown your strength in the past. What are some strengths that can help you now and into the future? Identify when you feel energized. A strength is something that energizes you, almost like a superpower. You can use strengths to help you in your life. The more you cultivate and use your strengths, the more powerful you can be in your life. Reflect on times of success to re-discover your strengths. Ask others for feedback about what they admire about you. Take one of the many strength-finding tests available. Everyone has strengths. Find the strengths that make you unique and powerful, then use them to your advantage.

Remember

You were made to do amazing things. True strength is keeping things together when everyone expects you to fall apart. Tap into your superpowers.

November 11

Be aware of your feelings.

*"Sad hurts, but it's a healthy feeling.
It is a necessary thing to feel."*
- J.K.Rowling

Today's message

Tell someone how you feel. Write how you are feeling in your journal. Listen to what you are feeling, as feelings are messengers. Many times, the messages that people are given are to hold in negative emotions. Growing up you might have been told not to cry. It is common to avoid unpleasant emotions at all costs. It is healthier to lean into your experience rather than to try and numb or avoid true feelings. When you numb sadness or any negative emotion, you can also numb joy and happiness. Processing and having feelings are a part of being human. The central part about being able to cope with emotions that are challenging is to practice self-compassion. Extend yourself kindness with all feelings. When you feel sad, anxious, or angry, be gentle with yourself. Experiencing emotions and being vulnerable is what makes you human. Check-in and ask yourself: How am I feeling? What do I need to express? How can I mindfully observe my feelings today?

Remember

You are human and being human means you have feelings. Feelings are a way of communicating.

November 12

Wire your brain for positivity.

*"Train your mind to see
the good in everything."*
- Old Saying

Today's message

Your strongest muscle that you can work is your mind. Whether you realize it or not, all the experiences, both good and bad, that you have lived through often influence your decisions. Your brain learns from difficult situations and painful memories. Your brain naturally wants to protect you so painful experiences don't happen again. It can become essential to train your brain to release the inner negativity holding you back. Train it well to see the good in every situation. Positivity is a choice. You can train your brain to flip negatives into positives. First, become aware when you are noticing negative, next retrain your brain to see the possible positives. You can take this step further and scan your day for positive things or list three good things. Pivot your negative thoughts towards the opposite or possible positive.

Ask yourself

What is the opposite of the adverse event? What is good and positive in my life? Where is the good in my life? What negative thought patterns need to be flipped?

November 13

Have faith.

"Everything you need comes to you in perfect time, space, and sequence."
- Louise Hay

Today's message

No matter what is placed in front of you, it's a part of your path. Faith is about having confidence in what you hope for and assurance even in what you don't see yet. It is essential to follow, trust, believe, forgive, and be grateful. Sometimes it takes the worst pain to bring about the best change. Train your mind to see the good in every situation and challenge. Having faith gives you strength and inner resolve even amongst struggles. Faith also gives you courage. Courage is the ability to do what scares you, to act on your beliefs despite threats, to show strength in the face of grief or pain. Faith makes you courageous. Having faith allows you to preservere through your day, offering stability even in the middle of instability. Faith brings comfort.

Remember

One day everything will make perfect sense. Have faith that everything will work out for the best. Perfect timing is the ability to turn a limitation into new, creative possibilities. It's up to you to find beauty in the ugly days.

November 14

Nobody is perfect.

*"Today, I will live in acceptance
rather than expectation."*
- Louise Hay

Remember
You don't have to like everything about yourself to love yourself. There will be things that bother you about yourself and things you wish you could change. But don't dwell on these things as they will only bring you down. There is freedom found in accepting however you feel at any given moment. You will thrive and move forward in a productive, peaceful, loving manner when you wholeheartedly accept the way you are. To accept yourself means not to deny or suppress what you are feeling but rather to acknowledge it. Feel positive about yourself and make it a habit to love and accept yourself daily. No one is perfect, and you are human. Take care of yourself, do your best, and enjoy your progress. Find approval from yourself, not from anyone else. If and when you accept yourself, you are inevitably setting yourself up to be happier.

Affirm
I love myself, flaws and all.
I choose to focus on my good qualities and strengths.
I re-route my thoughts of self-disapproval.
I love and accept myself daily.

November 15

Compete with yourself.

"If you compete with others, you become bitter. If you compete with yourself, you become better."
- Unknown

Remember

A challenge only becomes an obstacle if you decide that it is. Challenge yourself every day to do better and be better than you were yesterday. Knowing you have believed in yourself to set big enough stretch goals means you believe in yourself. Setting yourself goals requires self-worth, along with the belief that amazing things are possible for you. Competing with yourself every day also builds resilience, grit, and motivation. Avoid the temptation to compete or compare with other people. Put blinders on and run your own race. Remember, there is a delicate balance between being content and striving for more. Be ambitious and notice your development soar. Adopt a constant forward motion of bettering yourself. Mix acceptance into ambition while you are sitting with where and who you are.

Affirm

Every day I am getting better.
I see others as inspiration.
Today I challenge and accept myself.

November 16

Breathe deep.

"I will breathe. I will think of solutions. I will not let my worry control me. I will not let stress levels break me. I will simply breathe, and it will be okay."
- Shayne McClendon

Remember

A deep inhalation followed by an exhalation can change your body physiology from stressed to relaxed. Inhale confidence and exhale doubt. Take a deep belly breath, breathe into the abdominal area, or practice deep diaphragmatic breathing. Today remind yourself to take deep breaths. Your lungs expand and contract up to 20 times, but many times those 20 times are spent breathing into half of your lung capacity. Shallow breathing can deprive you of fresh oxygen. Deep breaths stimulate the parasympathetic nervous system, which helps the body relax and stay calm while helping with digestion. Train yourself to breathe slowly and deeply to prime your body to relax. Move out of the fight or flight response that comes with stress to a place of calm, clarity, and relaxation.

Affirm

Let me live, let me take a breath.
I love the feeling of fresh air in my lungs.
I stop and take a deep breath.

November 17

The new happy.

"Calm mind brings inner strength and self-confidence."
- Dalai Lama

Remember

It is commonly thought that happiness comes from physical things, stuff, money, or connections. But true happiness comes from authenticity, compassion, meaning, service, and joy. Many people say the expression: *I will be happy when ...* People often place their happiness on the acquisition of a particular event, situation, or accomplishment. The new happiness is more about the importance of accepting yourself, living your values, fostering your strengths, helping and being of service to others, looking for and appreciating the good around you, and doing the things that bring you joy. How can you strive to accept yourself, see your strengths, help others, be grateful, and do something you love today?

Affirm

I look inward and find my joy.
I choose to do things that light me up.
I am of service to others.
My strengths are_____, and I use them throughout my day.

November 18

Love yourself first
and decrease demands.

*"Self-love is not selfish;
you cannot truly love another until
you know how to love yourself."*
- Unknown

Today's message

How can you expect other people to respect you
when you push yourself and are hard on yourself? It
is common to feel burned out, exhausted, a lack of
purpose, and depleted. Be kind to yourself and
notice how paying attention to your needs feels
much better. Consider what your expectations are
for yourself. Release yourself from all the shoulds.
Look at your schedule and to-do list and ask
yourself: What can I let go of right now? Be honest
with yourself about how you are feeling. What
projects are not a priority right now? How can you
ask or be supported right now? Permit yourself to
take a break as well. Tap back into your strengths
and your gifts to help you with increased demands.

Remember

Pay attention to your burnout and high demands.
Hit the pretend delete or cancel button to lighten
your load. Talk to yourself like you are your own best
friend. Remember is it's okay to rest and ask for
help.

November 19

Take time to check-in.

"Sometimes when we get overwhelmed,
we forget how big our soul is."
- Unknown

Ask yourself
What is most important to me? What do I think is best for me? What resonates most for me? What am I needing? What am I feeling? What am I wanting?

Today's message
Take time to turn your focus onto yourself today. Be sure to listen to your own needs and what is important to you. Getting quiet allows you to hear yourself deeply. Life gets busy and chaotic at times; it is essential to step back and check in with yourself every once in a while.

Affirm
I honour my inner voice.
I trust my intuition.
I listen to my deepest desires today.
I take time to check in with myself.

November 20

Have some fun and play.

Love is that micro-moment of
warmth and connection that you
share with another living being."
- Barbara L. Fredrickson

Ask yourself

Can I think of a true friend in my life? How can I be silly and carefree today? How do I make people laugh, smile, and feel loved by being a friend?

Remember

Call on a friend to help you make your life beautiful. You deserve love and unconditional support in your life. Friendship is an all-in kind of thing. Do what makes you laugh. Be silly today. Think about what carefree children like to do and adopt a carefree inner child-likeness today. Do something that isn't adult-like. Drop and lie in the grass, do some finger painting, go jump in leaves. Have fun!

Affirm

I have lots of fun and play.
It's time to play and connect with a friend.
I am lovable and playful.
Today, I am spontaneous and joyful.

November 21

Be gentle with yourself.

*"Be nice to yourself; it's hard to
be happy when someone is
mean to you all the time."*
- Christine Arylo

Today's message

Being gentle with yourself means giving yourself
credit for what you have already accomplished. It is
about giving yourself a path of hope and excitement
of what is yet to come. Try not to be hard on
yourself. Notice when you are being mean to
yourself with negative self-talk. Recognize that you
are a human, growing, evolving, and learning every
day. By being easier on yourself, you will ease
pressure and stress. Remember that love is gentle.
To be gentle with yourself means to speak kindly to
yourself, to look after yourself, to be compassionate
with yourself, to take compliments, to manage your
schedule, to take a break, to do things that you love,
to get more sleep, to be gentle with others too, and
to get fresh air. What would being gentle with
yourself today look like?

Remember

There is an expression: *just when the caterpillar
thought the world was over, it became a butterfly*.
Be gentle with yourself; you are doing the best you
can.

November 22

Get outdoors.

"For one minute, walk outside. Stand there in silence. Look up at the sky and contemplate how amazing life is."
- Unknown

Remember

Log off and shut down all your technology for a chance to go outside. Getting outdoors can help to lift your mood and lower anxiety. When in nature, people tend to experience a more positive mood and better creativity and cognitive function largely impart to an increased oxygen supply. Nature helps you wake up and feel alive. It feels good to get lost in nature and be present in the moment where the real gifts are found. Albert Einstein said it best: *"Look deep into nature, and then you will understand everything better."* Fresh air, sunhine, and trees are magical and according to many studies can have strong healing powers. Get out to the beach, park, or forest today and notice the uplifting effects.

Affirm

Today, I enjoy the great outdoors.
I renew my spirit with nature.
I am part of nature, and I am beautiful.
I take deep breaths outdoors and feel energized.

November 23

Accept the things I cannot change.

"God grant me the serenity to accept the things I cannot change, courage to change the things I can, and the wisdom to know the difference."
- Serenity Prayer

Today's message

Trying to change things that cannot be changed can be very stressful and draining. As humans, psychological flexibility can be learned and cultivated. It is possible to open up to what is and accept the current situation and establish resilience. Inner peace comes from recognizing that you choose your emotions and how other people affect you. When you discover to let go of the things in your life that you cannot change, you will be at peace. Trying to change someone or a situation that you have no control over is a recipe for stress and distress. Choose peace in the moment you are in by accepting the things in your life that you cannot change. To enhance this acceptance, try to be in the present moment, open up to your feelings, embrace uncertainty, and focus on yourself and your values: what and who is most important? How can you express your values and needs, given the current circumstances?

November 24

Direct and focus your energy.

"The secret of change is to focus all of your energy not on fighting the old, but on building the new."
- Socrates

Today's message
A focused mind enables you to carry out everything faster and more efficiently. Today, direct your mind and focus your attention during your tasks, conversations, and projects. Focus is directed attention. When you focus, you are concentrating your attention and effort. It sounds easy, but it can be hard at times. Attention might wander away but simply bring it back into focus. Direct your energy to positive ways of thinking, and you will feel much more at peace and productive. When you focus on the good things in your life, you will feel confident and safe. When you practice directing your attention, you will gain the benefits of being productive and getting things completed.

Ask yourself
How can I be mindful and focused today? What are my main distractions? How can I limit distractions? What do I need to focus on today? What needs my undivided attention?

November 25

Be determined.

"No goal was ever met without a little sweat."
- Unknown

Today's message

There is so much motivation and grit when you stay true to what you desire in your life. Combine your passion with perseverance, and great things will happen. If you need skills to advance towards your goals, take the necessary training. Look into what you need to succeed. Let no one person or any obstacle stand in your way. In Angela Duckworth's research on grit, she demonstrates the power of grit for progress and how it's not all perseverance; you need passion too. We need to have sustained persistence towards long-term achievement. She talks about the importance of resilience, ambition, and self-control in the pursuit of goals. To be determined and to get more grit, combine your purpose, your practice, hope, and time. What can you do to have more grit and determination today?

Affirm

I am a strong and determined person.
I am committed to what is important to me.
I continue to strive and make things happen.
I keep enhancing my skills and practice.

November 26

Don't hesitate.

"Hustle isn't just working on the things you like. It means doing the things you don't enjoy so you can do the things you love."
- Unknown

Remember

Taking action is a beautiful way to remove any doubt from your mind. Taking action helps you overcome fears, and as you expand your comfort zone, you are more willing and likely to do things in your life that will benefit you and move you towards your goals. Constantly taking action, big or small, creates a positive upward spiral of belief, hope, and achievement. Believe in yourself and go for it. If something excites you and makes you a bit nervous as well, just go for it. Don't be afraid to try something new; you never know how much it could change your life. Action brings a sense of satisfaction and makes you prove to yourself what is possible. Action has the potential to clear up any doubt or confusion, while continually acting builds habits. You have probably heard the expression: *you are what you repeatedly do*. Don't hesitate today. Now is the time.

Affirm

The time is now for me.
Opportunities are knocking, now is the time.

November 27

You are getting there.

*"Ask yourself if what you're doing
today is getting you closer to
where you want to be tomorrow."*
- Unknown

Today's message
Each day is a beautiful learning opportunity. You will
not always be a huge success, and some days will be
challenging, but you are continually learning and
growing. Don't get discouraged when things don't
seem like they are working; you are getting there.
Notice where there might need to be a few tweaks
to your regular habits that can help you get to where
you want to be. Good habits are energizing.
Consider some essential daily habits for lasting
happiness and success: Plan ahead, visualize your
success, try something challenging, get good sleep,
wake up early, exercise and move daily, eat
healthily, show kindness, keep doing what is
working.

Affirm
I may not be there yet, but I am getting better
every day.
I am continually learning and growing.
I see my life as a classroom.
Each day is a new opportunity.

November 28

Don't let your thinking
hold you back.

*"The greatest weapon against stress
is our ability to choose
one thought over another."*
- William James

Remember

The limit of what is possible for you only exists in
your head. Your beliefs become your thoughts, and
your thoughts become your actions and habits. Until
you believe you have options, you'll continue to feel
stuck. Try not to look at life in terms of black or white
because there are many versions of grey hiding in
between. Think with options in mind and challenge
limiting thinking and you will move from excuses to
progress. Keep a journal of your thoughts. Identify
limiting beliefs or statements that have become
automatic. Identify beliefs that you want to work
with and overcome. What are the root sources of
those beliefs? Challenge your beliefs. Make a
possible new belief.

Affirm

I have many options.
I challenge any limiting thoughts.
I have an open mind.
I pay attention to my thoughts and beliefs.

November 29

Trust in hidden benefits.

*"Pain and suffering are the soil
of strength and courage."*
- Lurlene McDaniel

Today's message

There is a reward to any pain, and it is experience. It is hard while you are in the pain or suffering to see the potential gifts and learning, but strength will be born. Your resilience in dealing with adversity that seems like a burden soon will be the very thing that frees you and might even look like a miracle or blessing. There is an expression: *everything happens for a reason*. Take comfort in this idea. Create some time to have personal space for your soul to recover, rest, and think. Suffering is the school where your heart and soul can learn and become strong. See challenge as a way we are shaken up a bit that drives us to look at life differently and do things in a new manner. Trust that there are new opportunities amidst struggle, even if you don't see them yet.

Affirm

I am strong.
I learn and grow.
Tough times will end.
I see the challenge as a shake-up of my life.

November 30

Prioritize.

"Live your truth. Express your love. Share your enthusiasm. Take action towards your dreams. Walk your talk. Dance and sing to your music. Embrace your blessings. Make today worth remembering."
- Dr. Steve Maraboli

Today's message

What needs your complete focus and priority today? You can choose what gets your attention and the choice is entirely up to you. What needs your attention and effort today? You have probably heard the expression: *work smarter, not harder.* Establishing priorities is necessary to complete the things that need to be done. Prioritization is essential because it allows you to give your undivided attention and focus on a task. Take time to weigh the urgency and importance of tasks that need to be done. Order and assign your tasks with the amount of effort and time you think is required of you. Be realistic with your expectations for yourself. Let go of irrelevant tasks or wrong priorities. Put effort into refocusing and reprioritizing so you can stay productive and get important things accomplished.

Ask yourself

Which parts of my day require my total presence?

December 1

Let go of shame.

"The difference between shame and guilt is the difference between 'I am bad' and 'I did something bad.'"
- Brené Brown

Today's message

Shame is an unpleasant self-conscious emotion that typically comes from evaluating yourself in a negative light. The emotion causes you to withdraw and feel distressed. Shame is different than guilt. Guilt is a feeling you get when you did something wrong or perceived you did something wrong. Shame is a feeling you get when you feel embarrassment or humiliation that comes from perception. What would it look like if you were free of shame? How would you act if you were free of fear? When shame or fear shows up, take notice. Then get curious about those sensations. Where is it coming from? Loosen the grip by imagining yourself without those sensations. Move around with a sense of trust in yourself and the world.

Ask yourself

Do I shrink away from complex tasks or projects because of fear of discomfort? Do I hold back information out of fear of being judged? Do I procrastinate or get distracted and feel shame around laziness or lack of focus?

December 2

Be awesome today.

"Self-awareness is a key to self-mastery."
-Gretchen Rubin

Today's message

Don't be afraid of your power. Don't let anyone dull the sparkle that lies inside you. Take time to find your strengths and your weaknesses. Start by creating two lists. For yourself, identify your strengths and weaknesses without being too hard on yourself. You have the power to develop your magnificence. Once you create your lists personally, start talking to people you trust and ask them what they feel are your strengths and weaknesses. If there is something you don't like about your life, change it. Tap into the things that make you awesome. Self-awareness is the key to being awesome. Take time to know yourself deeper and find clues of your strengths, even in your failures. Analyze your successes and failures to find more information. Knowing your strengths and weaknesses helps increase your self-awareness and allows you to appreciate yourself as well as have a better grasp on areas to develop and grow.

Ask yourself

What are my strengths and weaknesses? How does knowing this information help me? What makes me awesome?

December 3

Simplify to amplify.

*"You get what you focus on,
so focus on what you want."*
- Unknown

Today's message

The more clear you are on what you desire and how you want to show up in this world, the easier it is to balance your life. When you simplify things in your life, it allows you to be more creative and feel lighter. Simplicity makes things easier. Sometimes people make things much more complicated than things need to be. By applying simplicity to life, you will make the complex seem simple. Thinking and being simple strips away the non-essential business and noise, allowing you to focus. With added focus, you can amplify the results you are looking to achieve. Simplify your life today. Simplify your career. Simplify your relationships. Simplify your environment. Think about what it is you desire most for yourself and get very clear on that vision. Take this opportunity to get rid of extra mental and physical clutter so you can focus on the things that matter most to you. See where you can simplify to amplify your life today.

Ask yourself

If it were simple, what would it look like? If it were easy, what would it be like? What do I want? What would be the best simple outcome?

December 4

No need to rush.

"Relax, everything is running
right on schedule."
- The Universe

Remember

Don't rush into things. Practice patience and keep a good attitude. Being rushed or feeling pressed can distract your attention and focus, making mistakes or stress more likely. Rushing through life trying to catch up or push motivation adds to stress with not that much benefit. Fear and the consequences of falling behind play a role in rushing, and the brain goes into threat mode. When you are in threat mode, you are pulled away from awareness, logical mental function, and calm. Rushing, therefore, makes you less productive. It is easy to feel behind. Be in the moment, cultivate awareness, and ask yourself: What is the worst that could happen if I act normally and don't rush? Take control of your schedule. Further to that, don't rush on anything. When the time is right, it will happen.

Affirm

I am patient and choose not to rush.
My life is unfolding as it should.
I take one thing at a time.
I take ownership of my time.
I pay attention and have faith in my life.

December 5

Detach emotionally.

*"When you finally let go of the past,
something better comes along."*
- Sonia Ricotti

Today's message
Emotional detachment can help you remain calm and undisturbed when people criticize you, when plans don't go as expected, or when you encounter upsetting situations or people. It means letting go of negative thoughts and emotions that might disturb you. Sometimes it will hurt to let go, but it may hurt more to hold on to the past or expectations. When you let go, you make space for something better. Further to that, to acquire something, you have to relinquish your attachment to having it. Detachment can be challenging. Being objective is powerful in practicing detachment. Become fully immersed in your life and the moment, but step outside and reflect on detaching. One step to detach is to notice where you are attached to an object, a goal, a dream, or another person. When you live your life from an internal place rather than connecting your ability to be happy on external conditions or people, you gain immense freedom.

Ask yourself
What do I need to detach from today?

December 6

Use feelings as guidance.

"Feelings are like waves. We can't stop them from coming, but we can choose which ones to surf."
- Jonatan Martensson

Today's message

Let your smile and happiness change the world, don't let the world change your smile. Emotions are a natural part of life. They really are not negative or positive. Instead, they are signals trying to move you in the right direction based on your values and beliefs. You decide what you put your attention onto. Honour your feelings and inklings as they are saying something to you to help guide you. When dealing with negative emotions, you can decode their signals to discover what problems need solving. You can effectively express negative emotions. Take notice of your emotions and allow them to guide you. You can either let the situation continue and keep those emotions or you can change the way you're reacting to the situation. You can change the way you are thinking about the situation. The bottom line is that all emotions are messengers, make sure you listen to them instead of sweeping them under the carpet. Feelings have immense value.

Ask yourself

What are my emotions telling me?

December 7

Personal breakthrough.

"Breakthroughs happen when limiting thoughts and behaviors are challenged."
- Fabienne Fredrickson

Today's message

Success comes when your continued persistence breaks through resistance. If you are prepared, you will be confident, and you will be ready to face opportunity. Until you spread your wings, you will have no idea of just how high you might be able to fly. If you are stuck in a rut and your life is not going exactly how you want it, you might want to encourage a personal breakthrough. It is beautiful when you have a moment that positively changes the course of your life in a new powerful direction. Something that might create a personal breakthrough is hitting a low point that requires some tweaking in your life. Take time to analyze the stories you have been telling yourself. Become aware of the possible lies you are telling yourself. Decide you want a personal breakthrough and plan. Your life is full of unlimited possibilities.

Remember

Ask for what you want and be prepared to get it. Your beliefs are like a magnet to create your reality. Drop or let go of limiting thoughts.

December 8

Take back your power.

"The way to have power is to take it."
- Boss Tweed

Today's message
Express your strengths. Don't let others define who you are and what your strengths and weaknesses might be. You are capable of anything. Stand in your power and connect with your strengths. You are unique, and not one person can be like you. That is your power. Choose to love yourself first and stick to your truth. Make sure you set boundaries for yourself and be the leader of your own life. Know there will be ups and downs as you flow through life but avoid negativity as much as possible. Try to own and use your strengths for your benefit and the benefit of the world.

Ask yourself
What would make me feel more powerful? What are my strengths? What are my superpowers? How can I get to know myself better? What boundaries do I need to set? What are my expectations? What makes me confident? How can I be more fearless?

December 9

More than just positive thinking.

*"A negative mind will never give you
a positive life."*
- Ziad K. Abdelnour

Remember

There is a difference between positive thinking and positivity. Positive thinking is more about telling yourself only to think or see the positive and pretend bad things don't happen. Positive thinking often gets a bad reputation. Positivity is more profound than that; when you are realistically optimistic, accepting the truth of reality, and are hopeful for a brighter future. It is about seeing and noticing the good in what could be challenging. What you think about is what you become and what you attract into your life. When you can practice positivity, you honour all emotions and events and choose to see the possible growth, opportunity, and or learning in each situation. You are better able to be grateful for all the gifts life might throw at you. Never underestimate the power of thought. Choose your thoughts wisely. Choose to embrace positivity.

Affirm

Today, I choose to embrace positivity.
I fill my life with positive energy.
I look for the good in situations.
I embrace all emotions and am hopeful for the future.

December 10

Relax and unwind.

"Sometimes you just have to stop,
take a deep breath and
put things into perspective."
- Katrina Mayer

Today's message

Take time to relax and unplug from your busy world. A tranquil state brings a feeling of freedom from agitation and stress. Taking time to relax and unwind helps you to have a calmer and clearer mind which can help in many aspects of your life. Relaxation and unwinding reduce the adverse effects of stress on the body and allow you to regain energy. Unwinding helps to down-regulate your nervous system by slowing down the heart rate and relieving tension. Make some time for yourself today so you can relax, reflect, and renew your spirit. Find the calm in the chaos by stepping out and pampering yourself. Relaxation is a skill you can learn and improve on with practice. Find ways to unwind and relax like yoga, meditation, walks, deep breathing, reading, taking a bath or sauna, listening to calm soft music, or use guided imagery.

Ask yourself

What helps you unwind? What is my best kind of relaxation? What can I do today to help me unwind and relax?

December 11

Believe the best is yet to come.

"Forget all the reasons why it won't work and believe the one reason why it will."
- Jon Chandonnet

Today's message

There is an expression: *Don't be pushed by your problems or any obstacles, be led by your dreams instead.* Today, tap back into your dreams and visualize them manifesting. Feel how it feels to have your dreams come true. Enjoy imagining the process to get you to your dreams. Believe and see what is possible for you. Always remember the future belongs to the people who see possibilities before they are apparent. Look for options and have faith in what will be.

Remember

You are braver than you believe, stronger than you seem, and smarter than you think. Take time to step away from life and restore your dreams today. Go back to that place where you hope for the best for yourself and think about how good you can stand it. You were given this life because you are strong enough to live it well. Don't be afraid to start over and have the chance to rebuild what you desire.

December 12

Practice appreciating.

"Gratitude dissolves negativity. Decide that no matter what comes your way, you'll find a grateful heart."
- Unknown

Today's message

Appreciation is a beautiful tool to help you see and notice what is positive in your life. Gratitude gives you the ability to see love, joy, and abundance. Appreciation allows you to see everything that is already right in front of you that is amazing. Take time to be thankful and express this gratefulness to those in your life. It is common to overlook the good things in your life. Pretend you got transported into your life and see it with fresh appreciative eyes. When you are present in the moment you are in, being grateful for what you already have, you will experience happiness and balance. Take notice today of all the miracles and blessings around you.

Affirm

I can find joy in my life when I look for it.
I have an extraordinary life.
I am so grateful for all the people and things in my life.
I value all the good things around me today.
I notice and savour all the good.

December 13

Remember how lovable you are.

"Good friends are like stars.
You don't always see them,
but you know they're always there."
- Old Saying

Today's message

Be sure to surround yourself with the people that make you happy, the people that make you laugh, those who help you when you need support. You want to surround yourself with people that know you are lovable. When you are with people that make you feel like you are hard to love, you need to make some changes. Choose to be around those friends that genuinely care about you. Remind yourself that you are lovable. Make yourself more lovable as well. They say that you become like the five people you spend the most time with. Since the people around us influence us, your circle of friends should encourage your growth and happiness. Be gentle with yourself and let your experiences be as they are with no judgment, just learning and development. Delve into what makes your soul happy and appreciate your strengths. Remember that you matter, and you are a special person. Remind yourself and find the people that remind you of that fact today.

December 14

Be understanding of others.

"Peace cannot be kept by force;
it can only be achieved by understanding."
- Albert Einstein

Remember

You never know what other people are dealing with, be patient and understanding. Compassion is a genuine understanding for others who might be struggling or experiencing hardship while having the desire to ease their pain. Hold back any judgment or critical thoughts towards others and try to understand instead. Don't hold onto your anger or bitterness as it is like drinking something poisonous. Choose instead to approach hurt with a loving heart. There are many ways to show compassion for others. The saying goes that if it comes from your heart, you are being compassionate. Start by being compassionate with yourself and express concern verbally and non-verbally. Offer encouragement to yourself and others, and don't be shy to express yourself. Act in thoughtful ways to yourself and others and know that we are all human.

Affirm

I am compassionate.
I show myself loving-kindness.
I am kind and offer support where needed.

December 15

Be proud and humble.

"Be like a pineapple: stand tall, wear a crown, and be sweet on the inside."
- Expression

Today's message

Own your truth and be confident. Remain humble and kind on the inside. When you are proud and humble, you can share your gifts with the world by accepting your strengths and limitations without defensiveness or judgement. Humility is a form of compassion for others and humanity. Being proud of yourself and your strengths is essential. Embracing your humanness is also powerful. One way to be proud and humble at the same time is to practice gratitude for your strengths and gifts while embracing humanity. See life as a journey forward, cultivating qualities that bring out the best in ourselves and others, making the world a better place. You can be confident and love yourself while being sweet and caring towards others all at the same time.

Affirm

I am proud of myself.
I am confident.
I love myself.
I am humble.

December 16

Visualize, imagine, and explore.

"Dream as if you have forever.
Live as if you have only today."
- James Dean

Remember

Daydreaming helps you believe things can get even better. Let the universe hear your dreams and get excited to see the magic that unfolds in your life. When you use visualization and imagination as a tool to explore possibilities, your brain is releasing a chemical called dopamine. It is a neurotransmitter activated when you encounter certain things in life that are linked to rewards. When you visualize success, love, accomplishments, and happiness, you will release that same hormone. Make sure you envision what you want and desire. Welcome each day with the joy and wonder of a child. Use visualization as a powerful tool that can help you get focused and move closer to your desired outcomes.

Affirm

Today, I awaken my inner child.
I step away from life and daydream.
I visualize, dream, and imagine.
I feel how it feels to reach my dreams.
I see the process involved with reaching my goals.

December 17

Be kind to yourself.

*"Never say anything about yourself
you wouldn't want to come true."*
- Brian Tracy

Today's message
Being kind towards yourself refers to acting in kind
and understanding ways towards yourself. It also
means talking kindly towards yourself. Your mind
and the inner critic are thinking thoughts and talking
to themselves regularly. Become aware of what you
are saying to yourself. Is it kind? Is it mean? Is it
funny? Talk to yourself like you would to someone
you love. The words we say to ourselves have
power, and they affect us tremendously. Halt,
pause, or delete voices that are negatively
impacting you. Alternatively, talk to these voices like
you are having a conversation. Let the voice know
you hear it and that they are trying to keep you safe.
Tell the voice why it's hurting you and ask for the
volume to be turned down a bit. Be aware of any
negative or mean things that you might say to
yourself. Add another voice that is your best friend
or advocate and listen to what that voice has to say.

Ask yourself
Am I hard on myself? What is my inner critic
saying? What voice can I add to the conversation?
How can I be kinder to myself today?

December 18

Let go of what is not working.

"Healing comes when we choose to walk away from darkness and move towards a brighter light"
- Dieter F. Uchtodor

Today's message

Give yourself time to heal. Sometimes it is essential to let go of something or someone to take back your power. Letting go is not forgetting, but rather it's remembering without fear and regaining your strength. Sometimes a part of healing is letting go of what is not working. Recovery does not mean that damage never existed or didn't take place. It means that it no longer takes hold of your life. Walk away from darkness and focus on what's good. Knowing when to let go can be challenging. You might need to let go if you are expected to sacrifice your values. You might need to let go if trust has been broken, or staying in it makes you feel broken, depressed, or frustrated. Sometimes it is common to cling on and hold on when it isn't healthy for you. Express yourself and talk through your thoughts and feelings. Take notice of inconsistencies, excuses, justifications, and your energy levels. If it's exhausting, that might be telling you something.

Ask yourself

What wounds do I have that need healing? What can I let go of to move forward?

December 19

Find calm in the chaos.

"Simplicity is the ultimate sophistication."
- Leonardo Da Vinci

Today's message

Never overlook the power of finding calm amid the chaos. When you are in the muck of struggle or challenge and your life seems chaotic, take pleasure in knowing you can find calm. Life will come with ups and downs and challenges. No one is exempt. Chaos and struggle are inevitable and a part of being human. It becomes essential to learn coping strategies around chaos. You have the power to reframe your thoughts to a view of possible growth and opportunity amid the chaos. One of the best ways to embrace struggle is to feel your feelings. Realize that feeling pain, sadness, anger, or fear is ok. You can search for possible benefits and plan for moving forward. Take note that you are human and that others also struggle. You are not alone, and it is a good idea to ask for and accept support. To help you find the calm you can take a walk, get out into nature, or journal your thoughts and feelings.

Ask yourself

What are the essential things in my life? How can I find calm amid the chaos? What helps me feel calm?

December 20

Notice varying energy.

"Where attention goes, energy flows."
- James Redfield

Remember

Take inventory of your day. Take notice of what is building you up and energizing you, and what is draining and depleting your energy. Simply take note and observe without judging. It is essential to realize that over time as you get upset, it drains you emotionally and energetically. It is also important to note all the things that energize you. That way, you can do more of what is energizing and less of what is depleting. Now is the time for better habits, positive thinking, eating clean, and loving yourself. Follow the things that energize and uplift, and minimize that which is draining. The higher your energy, the more efficient your body is, the better you feel.

Affirm

I am full of positive energy.
I take notice of my varying energy levels.
I do more of the things that energize me today.
I do less of the things that drain me today.
I practice energy-boosting activities.

December 21

Feel lighter today.

"Lighten up your mind and see the world lightened along with you!"
- Zara Humairc

Today's message

Purify your life today and do things that contribute to a feeling of lightness physically and emotionally. You can do some things to feel light: Keep your space, body, and mind clean. Clear clutter and overwhelm. Make decisions quicker and limit options to three. Develop a routine or program that supports you like yoga, meditation, supplements, water, and a diet rich in vegetables. Release what is no longer serving you in a good way; you'll feel lighter, and your space will function much better than before. Start habit tracking. Decide what habits make you feel lighter and track your daily activities with a mark in your calendar. Make some lifestyle changes that will help you to feel lighter physically. You can go on a mental cleanse too. Try to think about the thoughts that make you feel lighter. Keep things light today.

Ask yourself

What people or thoughts do I need to let go of? What things or activities help me feel light? What makes me feel light? When have I made space for me to be me?

December 22

Ease up and rest.

*"Do not confuse your bad days as a sign of
weakness. Those are the days you are
fighting the hardest."*
- Old Saying

Today's message

In life, as we go forward, there are times of mental
and physical exhaustion. Ease up on yourself so that
you can have freedom from discomfort, worry, or
anxiety. Have time to rest and enjoy leisure. Life gets
busy, and it is common to have high expectations.
But life can be and also needs to be fun. Easing up
on yourself means to treat yourself in a less harsh or
demanding way. Fatigue is different than being
tired. When you are tired, sleep can remedy it. But
if fatigue is still there when you wake up, and it stays
all day, it's time to take a much-needed break. When
your resources feel depleted, and you are pushing
yourself hard, balance expectations and pressure by
easing up on yourself. Give yourself permission to
take breaks and schedule them. Manage your time
and boundaries.

Ask yourself

How can I be nice to myself and ease up? What
would a break to restore my life look like? How will
I feel after I take a rest? What is something fun I
can do?

December 23

Create new routines.

*"Make it a great day or not,
the choice is yours."*
- Unknown

Remember

Try to go somewhere you have never been before. Make a new routine to shake things up in your life. Unless you try to do something beyond your comfort zone that you have already experienced, your life will not change. There is something called good stress and novelty. When you create new routines or experiences, you feed your brain and gain a sense of accomplishment through new learning. By changing up your routine and incorporating something fun or different, you can enjoy can bring about excitement and enjoyment to your day. Breaking the monotony and varying your routine is stimulating and good for your mental health. Life gets boring if you stay within the limits of what you already know. Try something new each and every day. Trying new things increases energy, motivation, creativity, and even productivity. Make a conscious decision to shake up your routine today and enjoy new experiences.

Affirm

I take a deep breath and break free.
New routines increase my energy levels.
Today, I try new things and I explore new ways.

December 24

Be gentle and kind.

"A gentle word, a kind look, a good-natured smile can work wonders and accomplish miracles."
-William Hazlitt

Today's message

When you share pieces of your heart with others, your heart grows more significant and more beautiful. Being gentle and compassionate is more than just giving treats or compliments. Being gentle to yourself and others is one of the foundations of happiness. It seems to be common sense that when you are kind and gentle towards others you are happier, but science confirms that our subjective well-being is higher when we also practice self-compassion and gentleness. Think about gentleness and kindness as more than just actions representing kindness. Instead, see them as actions that are kind and gentle that make you also feel kind and gentle. At first glance speaking gentle and kind to others might not seem to be about you, but research shows that being kind to others can make you feel happier. Deciding to be kind and gentle with others activates the reward center of the brain.

Ask yourself

How can I show up gentle and kind today? How can I care for others and feel loved? In what ways can I practice kindness?

December 25

Choose your battles.

"Be selective with your battles. Sometimes peace is better than being right."
- Unknown

Today's message
Choose gentleness today. Speak in a soft voice. Move-in a smooth slow manner. Decide to choose not to participate in minor, unimportant, or overly complicated arguments today. Save your strength instead for those things and people that will have a significant impact on your life. Choose smooth-motion activities like yoga. Listen to soft music. Let yourself be silent and turn inward. Learn to pick your battles, so you don't run yourself ragged. Try not to enroll in petty debates. Try not to engage in or participate in any fights. There are times when it is healthier to choose peace and turn inward. Choose what you participate in today.

Ask yourself
What would bring me peace today? How do I find calm? What makes my heart calm? Where do I need to be selective? How can I shift my focus? Is there something that I need to let go of today?

December 26

You're guided in beautiful ways.

*"If you're brave enough to say goodbye,
life will reward you with a new hello."*
- Paulo Coelho

Today's message

Being self-aware is not the absence of mistakes but rather the ability to learn, grow, and correct mistakes. You are guided in beautiful ways in life. Awareness allows you to get outside your mind and observe your guidance. There are many ways you can tell you are being guided. Detours in your life may lead to discovering places you never knew you would love. Pay attention to things that feel like prison versus wings. Do things feel heavy or light? Do things feel kind or cruel and insensitive? Does it excite, energize, or make you feel alive? Or does it exhaust or make you feel like you dread it? Does it nourish or deplete you? Does it feel natural, efficient, peaceful, and graceful? Does it make sense? Will it hurt anyone? Would you love to do this? How does it feel in your body? You are being guided in many beautiful ways. Be sure to pay attention and embrace guidance and potential.

Remember

Pay attention, as eventually, things fall into place. Trust in and listen to the guidance around you.

December 27

Journal your inner nudges.

*"Journaling is like whispering to oneself
and listening at the same time."*
- Mina Murray

Today's message

Journaling allows you to calm your mind and connect to your inner self. Journaling can help increase a positive view towards life, and fills you with more self-awareness and a feeling of autonomy or influence on your life. Keeping a journal can enhance your life in many ways. When you have inconsistent routines, unprocessed emotions, you feel stuck, or are running on autopilot, writing in a journal is a powerful tool to guide you along your journey of self-discovery. That is where your soul lives and the music is playing. When you are worried it's probably that you are trying to figure out everything on your own. When you write down your thoughts and inner nudges, you allow for healing, harmony, and clarity.

Ask yourself

Can I look deep inside my heart by writing in my journal? If everything lies within, how can I take time to look inside? What answers and guidance are found in the pages of my journal?

December 28

Know you are protected.

"May angels fly with you, wherever you roam and guide you back safely to family and home."
- Mary Jac

Today's message

All humans require protection. Sometimes you might feel fragile and need to feel protected. Protection and safety are fundamental human needs. This feeling might intensify when you are faced with a situation that is inherently risky or unknown. Mentally know that all the things you think about will be supported if they are meant to be. What you put your mental attention on, you will attract that thought into your life. You have the power to cultivate and strengthen these protective bonds in your life. Find ways to feel at peace, protected, and have faith. Reach out and create protective bonds with other people. Remember your self-care skills. Grieve where you need to and surround yourself with supportive people. Keep a gratitude journal and notice how you are already safe. Reach out and help others that need support.

Affirm

I am safe.
I am protected.
I am supported and resourceful.

December 29

Trust your desire for change.

*"Your desire to change must be greater
than your desire to stay the same."*
- Unknown

Today's message
Make way for something new in your life. It is not unusual to desire changes. Take a step back and look at why you might be seeking change. What isn't working and what needs changing? Why? It is essential to be honest with yourself about how you got to this place where you are currently. It takes courage to want change and try something new. Sometimes it is hard to make changes. It becomes necessary to trust your desire for change. There is a spark inside everyone. You just have to light it up and let that spark shine. Uncertainty and mystery are a part of life. Life changes may be scary and full of angst, but focus on what is possible once you make these changes.

Ask yourself
Why do I want this change? What are the risks in not pursuing this goal? Am I trying to impress someone? What precisely will I get as a result of this change? What is my intent in creating change? Who is best to help and support me through this change?

December 30

Be compassionate.

"Namaste: My soul honours your soul.
I honour the place in you where
love, light, truth, beauty, and peace reside
because it is also within me.
In sharing these things, we are united.
We are the same; we are one."
- Yoga Adage

Today's message
Consider that we are all connected as humans. We all have struggles, challenges, and heartaches. When we understand other's perspectives, we are better able to be compassionate and understanding of others. Compassion is your ability to experience what others might be feeling with a desire to help or be a part of the experience. True peace and love come from this place of understanding. Not only does compassion decrease suffering by helping those who need support, but also it can boost your bond with other people. Human connection makes us happier.

Affirm
I put good out into the world.
I am empathetic.
I support others and feel good while doing it.
I love myself and others.
I share in the human experience.

December 31

Enjoy knowing you're in loving care.

"Having someone help you doesn't
mean you failed.
It just means you are not alone."
- Johnny Iuzzini

Today's message

Sometimes accepting help is more challenging than offering service to someone. Life can be easier if you receive support from people. You can't do everything alone. Knowing that you are not isolated and that other people are experiencing a whole array of emotions provides a degree of humanity that allows you to relax and ease suffering. Take time to retreat and focus on how you can build your energy up for new exciting things. Reach out and know that you are cared for and supported. Through thick and thin, you are supported. No matter what you might be going through, there is someone who has gone through something similar. Knowing this can transform how you feel about your struggle and yourself. Knowing that you're not alone and that all humans struggle offers an acceptance of being vulnerable. Share and talk with others.

Ask yourself

Where do I need to ask for help? What can I do to rest and recharge? Who surrounds me and supports me? Who or what group can I reach out to?

A Final Note from the Author

My Wish for You

We can't control the direction of the wind,
but we can adjust our sails. - Adage

Life is beautiful, joyful, and at times, it can also be highly taxing or even painful. Every day may not be good, but there is something good in every day. It is my wish for you that you can tap into your power and make your life extraordinary. I want you to feel your worth, realize your greatness, and discover all the beauty you bring to this world. Despite the struggles you might find yourself in, I hope you find your resilience and ability to thrive or bounce back.

I often say life isn't going to be sunshine and rainbows all the time. Therefore, it becomes essential to take good care of your well-being. I hope that this book helps you when faced with the hardships that life might throw at you. I want you to meet life head-on, saying, "I see it honestly. I am suffering. And I care about myself." I hope that through the daily support, you can reveal your human spirit's capacity to persevere and discover more joy. My goal is that this book offers you an excellent source of loving support that while you endure the ups and downs that life brings, you know that you are not alone and that there are many things you can do to build yourself up.

Life has not always been easy for me, and I know it is a part of being human. However, facing adversity head-on while building my resilience became my lifeline. This book is my way of turning pain into purpose, supporting humanity while spreading hope and joy. I hope it helps you along this incredible journey back to you, your happiness, and your resilience while facing adversity so you can struggle well and live life happy.

Sending Hugs!

Love, Andrea

P.S. I have a special gift for you.
Please head to my website for the special self-care gift that is waiting for you!

P.P.S. Do not hesitate to reach out to me!
www.andreaseydel.com

About the Author:

 Through her book clubs, thriving Facebook community and top-ranked podcast, Andrea helps you live your life happily! Andrea is lovingly nicknamed "The Book Doula" as she has helped hundreds of leaders, coaches, and entrepreneurs tell their stories and give birth to their books. She believes books change lives.

Andrea holds a degree in psychology with post-graduate training in Positive Psychology, Non-Violent Communication, and Life Coaching. She is a Positive Psychology Practitioner, Resilience Coach, and Consultant, and a happily single mother of two teens, one fur baby, and one feather baby.

She can be reached at
www.andreaseydel.com

Live Life Happy

PUBLISHING

Live Life Happy-Publishing

Helping people painlessly give birth
to books that change lives.

Dear Reader,
Thank you for purchasing this unique book
and joining the **Live Life Happy Community**
of readers. We are a publishing company
that is committed to bringing positive,
supportive and well-being-enhancing
books to life.

As a welcoming gift, we'd like to offer you
free access to the **Live Life Happy Book
Vault**, which is full of resources and support

to help you live a flourishing life. You can gain access here: www.andreaseydel.com.

Finally, If you or someone you know has been thinking about writing a book, sharing a message or gaining credibility in an industry, I can help you painlessly give birth to your book. As a book doula and founder of LLH Publishing, I help make author *book-writing dreams come true*. Best of all, these books are changing lives, and your message can help others too. So don't hesitate to reach out and set up a Book Chat, and please stay in touch!

Sincerely,
Andrea Seydel
(The Book Doula)

Questions? Comments? Contact me at andrea.livelifehappy@gmail.com.

P.S. Books Change Lives: Whose life will you touch with yours?